Clarence A. (Clarence Augustus) Walworth, William Henry Burr

The Doctrine Of Hell

Clarence A. (Clarence Augustus) Walworth, William Henry Burr

The Doctrine Of Hell

ISBN/EAN: 9783741163906

Manufactured in Europe, USA, Canada, Australia, Japa

Cover: Foto ©Andreas Hilbeck / pixelio.de

Manufactured and distributed by brebook publishing software (www.brebook.com)

Clarence A. (Clarence Augustus) Walworth, William Henry Burr

The Doctrine Of Hell

The Doctrine of Hell,

VENTILATED IN

A Discussion

BETWEEN

THE REV. C. A. WALWORTH

AND

WM. HENRY BURR, ESQ.

NEW YORK:
THE CATHOLIC PUBLICATION SOCIETY,
9 WARREN STREET.
1873.

Entered according to Act of Congress, in the year 1873, by
THE CATHOLIC PUBLICATION SOCIETY,
In the Office of the Librarian of Congress, Washington, D. C.

PREFACE.

It must be borne in mind that the following correspondence was carried on in the columns of the Boston *Investigator*, an infidel journal, and consequently before a public which was, in the main, infidel. This was to me undoubtedly a great privilege, on the supposition that I cared less for the honors of a victory than for the opportunity to win over souls to the truth. To use such an opportunity with any prospect of success, it is necessary to study the infidel mind — especially the mind of candid and sincere infidels. I have felt that there is a class of persons to whom the idea of hell, such as they have been taught to conceive it, is the prominent and repulsive feature of religion. It is an easy thing to represent this aversion of theirs as being, in all cases, the result of an obstinate and perverse conscience that revolts at the thought of hell, because it craves the license to sin. But this is not true of all, nor can Christian teachers clear themselves from the labor and responsibility of argument in this way. Sincere men sometimes revolt from the doctrine of hell because it seems to them irreconcilable with the attributes of a good and merciful God, and with the best instincts of the human breast.

Such men, it may well be suspected, misunderstand the doctrine. If so, it is the part of a good Christian to meet them courteously, to hear them patiently, to search for the real difficulty as it exists in their minds, to grapple with it fairly, and endeavor to solve it by placing the question before them in its true light, and in terms intelligible to them.

The simple art of an earnest man is to address himself to the audience before him. In my letters to Mr. Burr, I have had in view the readers of the *Investigator*—infidels, and those whose connection with infidels brings them more or less under the influence of infidel ideas and infidel literature. I have therefore endeavored to "vindicate the ways of God to man," by showing that even in the other world, and when dealing with the hardened and reprobate, he parts with none of his eternal attributes; and that, if they are miserable, it is the necessity of their moral condition, and not because he has ceased to love and pity his creatures.

It will be noticed, moreover, that I have planted myself simply and purely upon the defined doctrine of the Catholic Church, and what that doctrine logically and necessarily involves. Why should I constitute myself the champion of anything more? And, least of all, why should I do this when dealing with souls outside of the fold, struggling with ignorance, prejudice, and the habit of unbelief—souls whom the Church would so gladly gather to her arms? Why should I make faith more difficult to them than it has been made to me and to the rest of the faithful? I have therefore steadfastly refused to defend any particularities whatever outside of the authoritative definitions of the Church. Of course, all the language of Holy Scripture on the subject must be accepted and maintained; but where the true meaning of that language is left undecided, it would be very unwise to risk my chances in a controversy by upholding hard and doubtful opinions, even if they coincided with my own.

If anything has been demonstrated by this discussion, it is this, that there is little headway to be made against the doctrine of hell when so presented. Almost all of my adversary's attacks were made against positions which I felt no call to defend. And yet I laid the whole essential doctrine before him in all its vast proportions, and in its full moral power—all the more vast, more solemn, and more telling upon heart and conscience, when the details of punishment are left covered by that mysterious veil in which eternity and the ways of God in eternity are necessarily clothed.

It seems scarcely necessary to give a reason why the usual proofs from the Bible have not been introduced. One of the litigants was an infidel, recognizing no revelation. To him, and to the readers of the *Investigator* generally, the testimony of the Bible is no authority, and it would have been a waste of words to bring it forward in this discussion. My only argument, therefore, has been to show the accordance of the Christian doctrine with the natural reason and conscience of man. Here lies the real difficulty in most minds. This cleared away, the rest of the road is comparatively easy.

I give this correspondence to the public in book form, at the desire of friends in whose judgment I confide, in the hope that it may sometimes serve an useful purpose when put in the hands of the candid though unbelieving sceptic.   C. W.

CORRESPONDENCE.

To the Editor of the "Boston Investigator."

MR. EDITOR: A friend has sent me your issue of last Wednesday (March 13), in which I find an article headed "A Spicy Letter from a Catholic Priest," with this editorial comment:

"'FATHER WALWORTH' DECLINES INFALLIBILITY.— Mr. Walworth, a Roman Catholic priest of some years' standing, has written a letter in which he says he must decline believing in the infallibility of the Pope. He adds;—"

Then follows the letter, the signature not being given. As I am the only priest of the name of Walworth in the United States, I am obviously the person intended by your remarks, and the supposed author of the letter.

Sir, your editorial does me great injustice. You mistake me for another man. I never wrote any such letter. On the contrary, I believe in the infallibility of the Pope, and, since it has pleased the late Council of the Vatican to define the doctrine precisely, I accept it in the precise terms of that definition. I have neither declined to believe it nor been tempted to do so. I mean to maintain it, please God, while my life lasts, with all the other doctrines of the Catholic faith.

As the circulation of such an article as yours is not only most cruelly injurious to me, but may give great pain to friends who are too far distant to find ready means to refute it, I trust to your justice and manliness to publish this denial, and, if other papers have copied it, they owe me the same reparation.

CLARENCE A. WALWORTH.

ST. MARY'S CHURCH, ALBANY, March 17, 1872.

To the Rev. Clarence A. Walworth.

DEAR SIR: Seeing your letter in the Boston *Investigator* of March 27, declaring your acceptance of the recent Papal dogma of Infallibility, I am prompted to address you a brief enquiry.

You and I were members of the same class at college. Just before graduating, we were both "converted" under the revivalist Elder Jacob Knapp. That we were both "soundly converted" I presume you do not doubt any more than I. Elder Knapp was fond of referring to yours as a remarkable conversion. But in the course of ten years, you had become a Catholic and I a Free-thinker. How I now regard my conversion under the revivalist, you can easily surmise; how you regard yours, I cannot. I shall, therefore, be pleased to receive from you an answer to the following questions:

Did you, at the time of your supposed conversion, "get religion"? In other words, Did you, at that moment, escape the "wrath to come," and secure your *post-mortem* salvation? Or was it all a delusion? If you did not get religion then, will you be kind enough to tell me when and how you got it?

Respectfully,

WM. HENRY BURR.

WASHINGTON, D. C., March 28, 1872.

To Wm. Henry Burr, Esq.

DEAR SIR: I feel no hesitation in replying to the communication which you have addressed to me through the columns of the *Investigator*, and trust that my answer may prove satisfactory.

The expressions employed by you of "getting religion" and "securing a *post-mortem* salvation" are objectionable phrases, and I cannot well use them without more explanation than seems to be at present desirable. Setting them aside, therefore, I will endeavor to give a plain answer to the substantial meaning of your enquiry as I understand it. I do not of course propose to argue the issues which lie between a Catholic's belief and an infidel's unbelief. Your communication evinces no further desire than to institute a comparison between our present and our past convictions.

The "conversion" you speak of, which took place, as you remind me, when we were classmates at college, and listened to the preaching of Elder Knapp the revivalist, is to me no "delusion." I look back to it with pleasure, and hail it as a happy reality. That many delusions existed in my mind at that time is certain enough. But equally certain am I that a real, substantial, and lasting impression was made upon me then which changed the whole current of my life. You ask whether I "secured my salvation" at that time. I consider no man's salvation *secured* except by perseverance until the end—*finis coronat opus*. The question touches somewhat upon those sacred privacies which do not belong to the public. This much, however, I may say—had death come then, I know of no good reason why I should not have met it with such hope of mercy as becomes a Christian penitent.

The ground which you have broken

makes it necessary to speak of myself, but I confine what I have yet to say to my intellectual life as a believer in the Christian revelation. That time which you have recalled was the turning-point of a life. Not that my faith began then, but that then I began to prize and cultivate what I had. Since then, whatever else you may say of it, my life has been one of sincere and unwavering belief. That revolution in my faith which your enquiry searches for—that revolution when I abandoned the religious convictions of my earlier life—*never took place*. This may seem strange to you, remembering that, having been reared by Presbyterians, I afterwards became an Episcopalian, and am now a Catholic. But I declare to you that I have never abandoned a single point of religious belief which I ever had. (I say of religious *belief*, by which I mean *positive doctrine*, for a negative doctrine is not a matter of belief: it is merely protesting against some positive tenet of faith—merely a refusal to believe.) I have cast away many prejudices of former days; I have accepted many things which I once did not believe; and thus the horizon of my faith has been enlarged. This transition of mind is never painful, for it is only following the natural law of growth. But I have never yet felt the shock of a lost faith; I have never been called upon to part with even one old and familiar religious conviction, and God grant that my soul may ever be spared such desolation!

Why, then, should I look upon that early "conversion" as a delusion? It was based upon a faith which I then had and still have. I look back to it with pleasure. I feel grateful to Elder Knapp for the part which he had in it. I look back with love and reverence, to my parents first, and, after them, to every voice that ever taught me to believe, or sought to rouse my believing conscience to its duty.*

* My answer to Mr. Burr's question must not be

How is it with you, my old classmate? When Elder Knapp knew us, you had a faith, I infer; and that faith probably covered as much ground then as mine. Now, you say, you are a Free-thinker. This cannot mean that you are free to think and say what you believe to be true; for in this sense I am as free in my thoughts as you. You mean, I suppose, that you will accept no external authority as a guide in matters of religion. This freedom would be embarrassing in every other science, and lead to ignorant

understood as an endorsement of Protestantism in any form. I do not look upon Protestant churches as channels of grace, or as having any divine authority whatever. They are merely human institutions, and owe their origin to rebellion against the Church of Christ. If I entertain hopes of the salvation of individual Protestants, it is because, by their baptism, by that portion of Christian doctrine to which they still hold, and by the living faith and love of God which is in them, they are members of the true Catholic Church, united by this lien to the *soul* of that Church, although unconsciously astray from her *body* or visible fold.—(C. W.)

presumption. May it not perhaps be the same in that deepest of all sciences which looks further than sight and sound can reach? Practically, I take it, you reject the whole Christian faith and all revealed religion. The result of your thinking in this direction has not been to build up anything, but to destroy. I pity you.

It may sometimes be a necessity to tear down and destroy. But to me it is always a sad thing. I would rather plant a new tree than uproot an old one. It is a mournful thing to see lying prostrate on the ground a noble trunk which many busy hands in nature, working long and patiently, have conspired to uprear, which has braved so many winters, bloomed so many summers, and sheltered and adorned the soil where it grew. More keenly still we feel the ruin, when, the stump being removed, we see how deeply the roots were fastened in the ground, how closely they clung to it, and how the bosom of the earth was rent in the parting. Is it not so with a religious conviction in the soul? Can an old faith, the growth of years, be uprooted there without causing pain, without leaving desolation? Once you believed in God as a living, loving, personal Being, who created you—in no idle mood to forget you afterwards, but—to cherish you as a Father. You believed that wondrous history of Bethlehem and Calvary which shows us so dear to God, and brings him so near to us. These convictions had grown up with the growth of your faculties, and, like a plantation of trees, had thrust down their roots, and spread out their branches, and become a part of your life. Can such a growth be removed without laceration of heart, without leaving behind it a desolation? And what have you now to fill the void?

You reply, I suppose, that the work, however painful, was necessary; that these things were superstitious errors, and, for truth's sake, ought to be eradicated. I have no occasion to argue that now and here; but from my soul I pity you. And I congratulate myself that the love of truth in me has never called for such destruction.

And in you, my dear sir, may it not have been a sad mistake? May it not be that some great and holy truths of Revelation taught to you have suffered in the teaching, have been coupled with errors, been colored by prejudice, been pressed out of shape to suit some harsh, false system—ay, been stripped of their flesh and blood by rash reformers, and thus deprived, in great part, of life and beauty? It may be that the Old Church, if you would let her tell her own story, in her own way, and have the patience to hear her through, would yet find sparks enough, amid the ashes of your early faith, to kindle a new fire, and substitute light for darkness and desolation. I subscribe myself with much interest,

Your sincere friend,
CLARENCE A. WALWORTH.

To the Rev. Clarence A. Walworth.

DEAR SIR: The kindly spirit manifested in your letter is commendable.

Twice you say you pity me. Pity implies knowledge of suffering; and as you have no evidence of my being at all miserable now, it follows that you pity me for what you suppose I am to suffer hereafter. Such is the effect of a belief in the dogma of hell-fire. The unhappiest part of my life was when I believed it; therefore, from personal experience of its influence on my own mind, I can truly say I pity you, for it is a miserable delusion.

You object to the expressions "getting religion" and "securing a *post-mortem* salvation." What more appropriate terms can be used? The former has been one of most frequent use among revivalists, for whose work in converting souls you even now feel grateful. The latter conveys the exact meaning intended—namely, happiness in a world to come. When objection is made to calling a thing by its right name, I always suspect something wrong in the thing itself.

You say that your conversion under Elder Knapp was no delusion, and that, had death come then, you know of no good reason why you should not have " met it with such hope of mercy as becomes a Christian penitent." In other words, I understand that then and there your faith began, which you have never lost, and which will secure your salvation, provided you " persevere until the end." The proviso smacks rather of the Methodist doctrine of falling from grace than of the staunch old Calvinistic dogma of final perseverance in which you and I were brought up, and to which you subscribed in the Thirty-nine Articles of the Episcopal Church. I am gratified with your very liberal interpretation of saving faith, which embraces all who were once soundly converted, and who persevere until the end, whether they belong to any church or not. Why not go a little further, and embrace conscientious back-sliders like myself, whose hope of happiness hereafter rests not on faith at all, but entirely upon good works?

In speaking of your conversion under Elder Knapp, I cannot quite reconcile your statement, "not that my faith began then," with a subsequent one where you say, "It was based upon a faith which I then had and have." It is pretty clear, nevertheless, that you date the influx of saving faith at that time.

The fundamental fallacy of your logic is in the assumption that religion is a science—ay, "the deepest of all sciences." Religion lacks the first element of science. Even the word itself is undefinable, hence the many contradictory definitions of it by those who claim to be religious. What wonder, therefore, that many like yourself accept external authority as a guide where there is nothing scientifically established? Religion and science may yet be harmonized, but not until the former can be accurately defined.

You tell me I once believed "the wondrous history of Bethlehem and Calvary." Did you ever examine the historical proof of those stories? Are you aware that they rest solely upon anonymous, unauthenticated, incredible, and contradictory writings? The story of the miraculous conception is too absurd for belief. That of the crucifixion might be true, but it is quite certain that John discredits the story told by the other three Evangelists. All four, it is true, agree in fixing the day of the crucifixion on a Friday; but, while the first three make that Friday a passover day, John does not, but the day before the passover (John xiii. 1, 29; xviii. 28; xix. 14, 31, 32), which must, therefore, have been a Friday of another week. This and other flat contradictions by John of the other three Evangelists throw strong doubt upon the event itself, which is not supported by a scrap of contemporaneous history.

As regards that reverential word "Calvary," supposed to be the name of a hill where Christ was crucified, are you aware that there was no such hill and no such name? In the Greek, it is simply "place of a skull"—*kraniou topos*—which, being rendered into Latin, is *calvariæ locus*, whence the audacious translators of the Douay Bible have derived the word "Calvary." It occurs in each of the four Gospels, but the Protestant translators only dared to insert "Calvary" once, (Luke xxiii. 33), and that is corrected in the margin.

In conclusion, you ask me to listen with patience to the story which the old Church will tell in her own way, hoping that in it I may find light. I know too much already of the true history of the old Church ever to become a convert to it. While it held sway over Europe, darkness and desolation prevailed, and civilization took refuge under the sceptre of Mohammed until the dawn of Protestantism and the invention of the art of printing. Papacy was always the foe of civilization. For a thousand years, it overshadowed Europe like poisonous Upas-tree. It is now dying, and I hail the day when it shall no longer cumber the ground, but shall be rooted up to make way for useful vegetation. Then shall the desert rejoice and blossom abundantly, humanity "shall obtain joy and gladness, and sorrow and sighing shall flee away."

Your friend and brother,
WM. HENRY BURR.

To Wm. Henry Burr, Esq.

DEAR SIR: Although I have good reasons to desire all the rest that duty will allow me, the interesting nature of its contents will not suffer me to fail in replying to your courteous letter of the 27th of April. In it you touch on several subjects which I would gladly dwell upon. Not to abuse the liberality of the editor of the *Investigator* by making my reply too long, you will permit me for the present to confine myself to one.

You say: "The fundamental fallacy of your logic is in the assumption that religion is a science—ay, the deepest of all sciences. Religion lacks the first element of science. Even the word itself is undefinable, hence the many contradictory definitions of it by those who claim to be religious."

When I said that religion is a science, I

spoke of it in the *objective* sense, meaning that body of sacred truth which is our light and law to guide and govern us in our relations with God. This body of sacred truth, when presented to the human mind, is subjected in time to the same process which all truth must undergo to which we have access, namely, it is gradually analyzed, classified, compared with other known truths, becomes the subject of discussion, its terms are defined, etc., until it assumes the character and proportions of a human science. So dealt with, it becomes theology, or the science of religion. I call it a human science, because it takes the form or mould of the human mind, remaining, however, in its substance or essence what it was from the beginning—divine truth. In the same way, mathematical truth is not created by the human mind, but exists independently of it; and yet, when investigated, ordered, and classified by the human mind, it becomes the science of mathematics, and considered, not in its essential, but in its scientific character, it is the product of human intelligence, and therefore a human science. Science, true science, changes no truth, makes no truth, but only classifies and illustrates it.

I cannot allow either myself or my Church to be made responsible for any want of scientific character that you may allege against non-Catholic doctrine ; but I promise you that, when you challenge a Catholic priest to give a reason for the faith that is in him, you will find that he can give you settled definitions, logical method, and all the advantages that belong to an established science.

That religion as I have defined it is the deepest of all sciences appears from the nature of its subject-matter. There are those who deny that the natural sciences so-called are, properly speaking, sciences at all, since, instead of proceeding from known original principles to particulars, they are the deduction of principles from particular facts, and thus involve the logical fallacy of making the conclusion greater than the premises. How, it is asked, can one derive an universal law from any number of observed facts, since, however numerous, they are always limited in number, and therefore not seen to be universal? I myself am well satisfied with the practical moral certainty which belongs to carefully conducted natural science; and I only state the objection to show how much more profound are the other sciences—jurisprudence, which proceeds from authoritative statutes, combined with the original and immutable principles of justice; mathematics, which proceed from self-evident axioms; or metaphysics, whose problems are still grander, and whose principles deeper. While religious science, or theology, is broad enough to extend to all the various methods of thought, it is the profoundest of all; it is still more profound even than metaphysics, in the sense that it deals with many deep questions that philosophers never before handled, and solves doubts that they never before could solve. No man, for instance, can open Cardinal Cajetan's edition of the "Summa of St. Thomas Aquinas," where the notes of the editor are profounder even than the wondrous text, without appreciating this. I will only add here that sacred doctrine, or theology, amongst other things, investigates and solves those deepest problems of the human mind otherwise unanswered—What am I? Whence am I? Whither am I going?

> " Thou art the unanswered question ;
>   Couldst see thy proper eye,
> Always it asketh, asketh,
>   And each answer is a lie.
> So take thy quest through Nature;
>   It through thousand natures ply ;
> Ask on, thou clothed eternity !
>   Time is the false reply."

Ay, so it is. And yet human science;

untutored by religion, can give no better answer. Ask of it what eternity is, and for an answer it gives us only: Time without bounds. "By repeating the idea of any length of duration," says Locke, "with the endless addition of number, we come by the idea of eternity." Do we indeed? I should be sorry to commence repeating with the idea of ever arriving at any such result.

> "Dull Sphinx, Jove keep thy five wits!
> Thy sight is growing blear."

Conscious, however, of her incapacity to read her own riddles, the Sphinx concludes:

> "Who telleth one of my meanings
> Is master of all I am."

This sacred science does. Travellers from eternity to eternity, she tells us what we are, whence we came, whither we are going, and what is the meaning of our life. And thus she earns her glorious title of Queen and Mistress of the Sciences.

I have but little space left to say more. In my next, if it should be agreeable to you, I am ready to discuss another question which you have started, namely, that of future punishment, and would be glad to hear your objections to it more at large. I leave this, however, to yourself. I feel no disposition to dictate the course of our debate. All I ask is that it shall run upon those more primary questions which form the debatable ground between Christianity and infidelity. Infidelity strikes at the foundations of religion. In defending her, I wish to take my post near those foundations, leaving it to others to guard the superstructure.

One word more in the way of friendly explanation. You say you are gratified with my liberal interpretation of saving faith, which embraces all who are truly converted to God, provided they persevere; and you ask, " Why not go a little further, and embrace conscientious backsliders like myself, whose hope of happiness hereafter rests not on faith at all, but entirely on good works?" I answer that I would joyfully embrace you also if your good works were what we mean in theology by good works, namely, good works proceeding from divine charity, or the love of God above all things. But this can only proceed from a supernatural and living faith, "*fides formata caritate,*" and this you would not allow me to attribute to you. I am, however, no bigot, but ready to acknowledge all good wherever I find it. I can recognize good qualities in infidels—qualities which are good by natural endowment and by cultivation, although not elevated to a supernatural platform, and made divine by grace. I can recognize in them noble dispositions, amiable and attractive traits of character, and love them therefor. Do you suppose, for instance, that I do not admire, that I see nothing good in, such men as Agassiz and Emerson? These may both be called infidels, and, I trust, without offence. I understand the first to deny all revealed religion, although he recognizes the creating hand of God in nature, and speaks of it with an accuracy of conception and a beauty of expression that no clergyman can surpass. The other, a pantheist, speaks often enough of God, though what he takes for God is but the divine shadow. And yet so deeply philosophical is his mind, and in his study of nature so keenly conscious of a living breath behind the canvas, that he seems to me like a blindfolded genius groping after God, and only failing to grasp him when his hands are just upon him. I can adopt many of his verses to express some of the grandest truths in Catholic theology, as, for instance:

> "The fiend that man harries
> Is love of the best;
> Yawns the pit of the Dragon,
> Lit by rays from the Blest."

This aspiration after the highest Good (God) which exists in every man, without which Good his soul can never be at rest—this substitution, through the blindness of passion, of the imperfect and created for the all-perfect and uncreated Good, which in truth (philosophically stated) constitutes sin—all this is a familiar thought in theology, albeit nowhere more beautifully expressed than by Emerson. When I say, and from my heart, that I both admire and love these two representative men, I trust you will not accuse me of limiting my charity through any narrowness of mind or contracted sympathies of heart.

I remain, dear sir, in all brotherly kindness,

Yours truly,
C. A. WALWORTH.

To the Rev. Clarence A. Walworth.

DEAR SIR: Your attempted definition of religion as "that body of sacred doctrine which is our light and law to guide and govern us in our relations with God," is an illustration of the truth of my assertion that "the word itself is undefinable, hence the many contradictory definitions of it." Why "*sacred* doctrine"? Is there any *profane* doctrine that is not false? Your definition may pass muster among Catholics, and possibly among a few Protestants. It does not agree, however, with that of our lexicographers, nor do the latter very well agree between themselves. The best attempt to define the word that I have seen is that of the Editor of the *Index*, who says that "religion is the effort of man to perfect himself." So you see we are not likely to agree as to the meaning of the word, especially as you confound religion with theology, and say "that sacred doctrine or theology, amongst other things, investigates and solves those deepest problems of the human mind otherwise unanswered —What am I? Whence am I? Whither am I going?" Most emphatically do I deny that theology solves either one of these questions, or even that it sheds upon them one solitary ray of light. The only gleam that I have been able to discern comes through modern spiritual phenomena. These *seem* to prove a future life. But if they do not, then I find no evidence of continued existence, and death must be an eternal sleep.

I am glad to see you draw on the naturalist and the pantheist for the conception and expression of "some of the grandest truths of Catholic theology," such as you say "no clergyman can surpass." Though I cannot discover much if any light in Emerson's or Agassiz's theology, I nevertheless rejoice at your

The Doctrine of Hell. 41

recognition of such "Infidels" (so you call them, without offence) as teachers of Catholic religion. If I could believe that you spoke the sentiments of priests in general, I would say to Brother Seaver and all his coadjutors, "Lift up your heads, for your redemption draweth nigh."

You wish to discuss with me the question of future punishment, and would be glad to hear my objections thereto. You shall have them.

The first sermon I ever heard Elder Knapp preach (perhaps you heard it too) contained a description of hell which I cannot easily forget. It was in substance as follows:

"At a depth of less than one hundred miles beneath our feet, the vast interior of the earth is supposed to be a solid (!) mass of liquid fire. Imagine a portion of the earth's crust removed so that you could look down into the fiery abyss. Picture to yourself a multitude of lost souls doomed to dwell for ever in those everlasting flames. Tossed on the billows of that lake of fire, they cry out in the agony of despair: 'How long, oh! how long am I to suffer these torments?' And the voice of Jehovah answers in awful tones: 'Eternity has not yet begun to waste.'"

These words had their effect upon my young mind, as they (or similar ones) did upon yours, for before many days we were both numbered among the "brands plucked from the burning." I thought I believed in some such hell then. I do not now. Do you?

Take another conception of future punishment which prevailed among our pious New England forefathers. From the year 1662 for more than a century no book except the Bible was so much read in this country as the "Day of Doom," a poem by the Rev. Michael Wigglesworth. It was hawked about like common ballads, was taught with the Catechism, and may therefore be regarded as a fair exponent of the popular theology or religion of that time. I quote two stanzas:

> " But who can tell the plagues of hell
>   And torments exquisite?
> Who can relate their dismal state,
>   And terrors infinite?
> Who fare the best and feel the least,
>   Yet feel that punishment
> Whereby to naught they would be brought
>   If God did not prevent.

> " The least degree of misery
>   There felt is incomparable;
> The lightest pain they there sustain
>   Is more than intolerable.
> But God's own power from hour to hour
>   Upholds them in the fire,
> That they shall not consume a jot,
>   Nor by its force expire."

Such was the doctrine of future punishment taught in New England one hundred years ago by a class of clergy at least as far advanced in civilization and humanity as those of any other country. But, what is more appalling, this kind of punishment was to be meted out even to infants who had never personally transgressed—

> "But from the womb unto the tomb
> Were straightway carried."

This horrid doctrine has been preached within the memory of men now living. Doubtless it can be more than matched in the old theological literature of your Church. But it is no longer believed. Indeed, little is said nowadays about hell and future punishment at all. The doctrine is irrational, and humanity is fast outgrowing it. Suffering is a necessary incident to our existence, but the higher we rise, the less, it seems to me, must be its degree. If we are to live again, surely we are not going to suffer more than we do in this life. This incidental suffering is not punishment, but a beneficent provision of our being, without which progress would be impossible. In

the vindictive sense, I do not believe in any punishment at all, present or future.
    Yours truly,
        WILLIAM HENRY BURR.

To Wm. Henry Burr, Esq.

DEAR SIR: You seem to forget that religion, like faith, hope, science, infidelity, and a great many other things, may be regarded either *objectively* or *subjectively;* either as something exterior to the soul which the soul has to deal with, or as the soul's own attitude in regard to that thing. Thus Webster gives us both senses of religion well enough when he says: "It therefore comprehends *theology* as a system of doctrines or principles, as well as *practical piety.*" This confusion of ideas is of course an oversight on your part, for I cannot suppose you would wish to make capital out of the popular ignorance of such necessary distinctions.

And now for the question of future punishment, which I enter upon very gladly, for the reason that it seems to stand out in your mind as something especially repulsive in religion. Let me repeat, however, once more, that I will not on this or any other question allow myself to be held responsible for any definitions or notions of Elder Knapp, Rev. Michael Wigglesworth, or any other man or class of men, Protestant or infidel. It is a part of my vocation to oppose their errors, not to defend them; although I will cheerfully recognize anything good or true coming from them or any other quarter. I am a Roman Catholic. I accept the doctrines at any time defined by that ancient Church which I hold to be the only Church of Christ upon earth; and, where any questions remain undefined, I bow respectfully to the concurrent opinions of her leading theologians. Beyond this I will not be bound, and I beg you will cease to quote the adversaries of the Catholic Church as authorities for me.

You do not state your objections to the existence of a hell very distinctly, but I infer from the general tenor of your words that you find in it something inconsistent with the goodness of God. It shall be my business to show the contrary. I love God because he is good. I could not love him if he were vindictive or cruel. When fair and reasonable men raise such objections, I take it for granted that they misconceive the true Christian doctrine of future punishments. Let me therefore state what it is.

It is impossible to have any clear and adequate idea of hell without a correct notion of heaven. That state of final beatitude which we call heaven consists in the everlasting vision of God. There, as the Apostle tells us, we shall see him as he is, and face to face. This is not a natural state. No conceivable perfectibility of man in the natural order could ever attain to it. It is something supernatural, that is, a gift above and beyond man's nature. It lies in a higher plane. For this supernatural end, nevertheless, man was created. It is his original

The Doctrine of Hell.

destiny, God's ultimate design in his creation reaching not only beyond such happiness as is attainable in this life, but also beyond the range and scope of his natural powers in any future life. To reach this supernatural vision of God is heaven, is salvation. To fall short of it is hell, is perdition. This is the main and essential idea of hell, whatever other pains may be incidental to that state. When in discussion we lose sight of this cardinal idea, we only "darken wisdom by words without knowledge." And now, to enforce and impress this as the only essential and constituent idea of hell, let me illustrate.

Suppose that one of our race in the world to come should find himself deprived of the vision of God, and therefore of that supernatural bliss which constitutes heaven. Suppose, however, that he should still be happy thus far, namely, should be free from every species of physical pain, and should enjoy a happiness which, although confined to the natural reach of his faculties, should nevertheless be perfect and complete in its kind, and far beyond anything which this present world can afford. And finally, suppose that this happiness should be confirmed to him for ever. Would this be heaven, or anything like it? No. It would still be hell. It would be a lost destiny. And yet it would be a greater felicity than the most progressive infidel has ever dreamed of. Such a state could not argue cruelty on the part of God, unless infidel doctrine be confessed as still more cruel.

Now, strange to say, Brother Burr, this supposition is no fancy of mine. This is precisely the state which Catholic theologians, such as St. Thomas Aquinas and all the great masters of scholastic theology, attribute to little infants who die without baptism, to unchristened idiots who have been such from birth, and to all other human beings who, like these, may be

The Doctrine of Hell.   51

supposed to have died in original sin without any actual transgression of their own. Such is the cruelty of Catholic doctrine! These unfortunate beings are better off in our hands than in yours, Brother Burr.*

Of course, it is very different with those who are not innocent of actual sin. They incur something more than this penalty of a lost destiny. In proportion to the degree of their sinfulness they deprive themselves also of natural happiness, and incur positive punishment. Since, moreover, man is a mixed being composed of soul and body (both pertaining to the

---

* "The little unbaptized infant is not a vile and hateful thing in the sight of God. It is merely disqualified for the beatitude of heaven. It is innocent, good, beautiful, admirable, a masterpiece of creative wisdom, and loved by God."—" The grace of regeneration is a pure and simple boon from God to those who receive it, to which they have no claim. Those who miss it, without any fault of their own, are not injured, for they are not deprived of a natural right, but a gift of grace."—*Studies in St. Augustine, by Rev. A. F. Hewit*, ch. iv.

integrity of his nature, and both taking part in sin), both must share, also, in the punishment. Why should not all this be? Shall human laws involve the necessity of punishment upon the transgressor, and not the laws of God? Shall the laws of nature, so called, require obedience under penalty of pain, both mental and physical, and the moral laws of God involve no punishment? We see that the eternal laws of justice are not adequately vindicated in this life. Happiness is not meted out to the virtuous in proportion to his virtue, nor penalties visited upon the wicked in proportion to their wickedness. This must therefore be done in the other world. There justice must be established, innocence be manifested, sin be punished, wrong be made right, and the laws of God be vindicated. This is in accordance with the natural conscience of man, and therefore the heathen of all ages have held it with great unanimity. Celsus, a heathen philosopher of the second century, attacked the Christian religion most bitterly, as infidels attack it now, and published a book against it called "The Language of Truth." He did not venture, however, to attack the doctrine of hell. "Christians are right," said he, "when they think that those who live holily will be rewarded after death, and that the wicked will undergo eternal punishments. And besides, they hold this sentiment in common with the rest of the world."

Plato, too, after teaching the same doctrine in his *Gorgias*, makes this noble and animating appeal: "I call you back to virtue. I urge you to this holy combat, the greatest, believe me, that we have to sustain on this earth. Do battle, then, without ceasing, for you will be able to aid yourself no longer, when, standing before your Judge all trembling and affrighted, you shall wait to hear your sentence." Ah! my old friend and classmate, if you reject our Christian oracles in this matter, listen at least to these heathen authors who speak the language of natural reason, of conscience, and echo the testimony of the human race in all ages.*

Yours truly,
C. A. WALWORTH.

* See Appendix on the unanimous testimony of all ages and all races to the doctrine of hell..

To the Rev. Clarence A. Walworth.

DEAR SIR: It is the undefinable nature of the word *religion* which causes confusion of ideas. In Webster's Unabridged Dictionary of 1847, the following prolix definition is given:

"*Religion*, in a comprehensive sense, includes a belief in the being and perfections of God, in the revelation of his will to man, in man's obligation to obey his commands, in a state of reward and punishment, and in man's accountableness to God; and also true goodliness or piety of life, with the practice of all moral duties. It therefore comprehends theology as a system of doctrines or principles, as well as practical piety; *for the practice of moral duties without a belief in a divine Lawgiver, and without reference to his will or commands, is not religion.*" (!)

No wonder that Professors Goodrich

and Porter, in revising Webster's Dictionary, thought it best, in the enlarged and unabridged edition of 1864, to *abridge* this definition to the following small dimensions:

"The recognition of God as an object of worship, love, and obedience; right feelings toward God as rightly apprehended; piety."

You quoted a part of the earlier definition to show that religion comprehends both theology and practical piety. In the later definition, you will observe that theology is substantially, if not entirely, eliminated. Furthermore, two of the five meanings given in the old edition are stricken out in the new. These changes are significant. Theology is no longer a part of religion according to our latest dictionaries. What further progressive change will the next lexicographers make? How long before even God will be eliminated from religion? I see signs of it already. Theodore Tilton, while yet editor of the *Independent*, gave the word a new definition with God left out; and Francis E. Abbot, editor of the *Index*, followed with a similar definition which I gave in my last. Both these talented young men spoke as editors of religious newspapers and as religious men. When some such definition as theirs shall be accepted, religion and science, like the lion and the lamb, may lie down together.

In your first letter to me you said: "I declare to you that I have never abandoned a single point of religious belief which I ever had," meaning thereby, as you added, belief in "positive doctrine." That seemed to me a strange confession from one who was bred a Protestant, converted under a revivalist, and who afterwards embraced the Roman Catholic faith. Therefore, as a test, I submitted the doctrine of hell as taught by Elder Knapp and Michael Wigglesworth, which was certainly "positive" enough. But, lo! you object, and beg me to cease to quote the adversaries of the Catholic Church as authorities for you. Well, then, I will try you with a Catholic authority. A recent catechism has been published in England, written by a priest named Furniss, printed *permissu superiorum* and recommended to be used in Sunday-schools. It is called "The Sight of Hell." I quote from it the following:

"Little child! if you go to hell, there will be a devil at your side to strike you. He will go on striking you every minute forever and ever without stopping. The first stroke will make your body as bad as the body of Job, covered from head to foot with sores and ulcers. The second stroke will make your body twice as bad as the body of Job. The third stroke will make your body three times as bad as the body of Job. The fourth stroke will make your body four times as bad as the body of Job. How, then, will your body be after the devil has been striking it every moment for a hundred millions of years without stopping?"

Again: take this as a lesson to a girl of "perhaps about eighteen years old":

"You do not perhaps like a headache. Think what a headache that girl must have! But see more. She is wrapped up in flames, for her frock is on fire. If she were on earth, she would be burned to a cinder in a moment. But she is in hell, where fire burns everything, but burns nothing away. . . . She counts the moments as they pass slowly away, for each moment seems to her like a hundred years. As she counts the moments, she remembers that she will count them for ever and ever."

After citing Knapp and Wigglesworth on hell, I remarked that they could doubtless be more than matched in the old theological literature of your Church. I did not expect to be sustained by so recent a Catholic authority. The catechism, I am informed, has been issued within the last year or two in England, and a copy has been ordered for the Congressional Library. My quotations are taken from the Manchester (English) *Examiner*.

To reach the "everlasting, supernatural vision of God," you say, is heaven and salvation ; to fall short of it is hell and perdition. Upon actual sinners you believe there will be inflicted positive punishment pertaining to soul and body, but you forbear to indicate your conception of the degree of suffering, as Knapp, Wigglesworth, and Furniss have done.* Does

---

* Surely it is hard to indicate the degree of suffering where degrees must vary as widely as the degrees of criminality. Our Lord said of Judas: "It were better for that man if he had not been born." We are scarcely warranted to apply this language to all who are lost ; for, according to St. Augustine, not by any means the mildest of theologians, "the Lord said this not of all sinners, but of the most criminal and impious" (*Cout. Julian, Pelag.* v. 44). Some conception may be formed of a dividing point like this, where existence is more of a burden than of a blessing ; but

not your kindly cultured nature revolt at anything approaching the horrors these men have portrayed? Is not this apparent from your description of the future state of unbaptized infants and unchristened idiots, who, though condemned to hell, "enjoy a happiness" which is "perfect and complete in its kind, and far beyond anything which this present world can afford"? Personally I would prefer your hell for infants and idiots to your heaven for saints, for I fear that I should prodigiously get tired of the "everlasting vision of God." But I beg to correct your assertion that your hell for infants "would be a greater felicity than the most progressive infidel has ever dreamed of." We have a noted brother in our ranks, Andrew Jackson Davis, who, while yet a boy, being put into a magnetic sleep, dictated a most remarkable work called "Nature's Divine Revelations."

who will undertake to measure out degrees of misery on either side of such a zone? C. W.

Call it a dream if you will, but in that dream you will find a description of heaven for infants that I venture to say far surpasses any conception of Thomas Aquinas or any of your great masters of scholastic theology.

You commend me to Celsus and Plato, if I reject your Christian oracles. Unfortunately, your Christian oracles burned the works of Celsus, and all we know of him is what his artful antagonist Origen chose to give. Plato was a good tutor in his day, and Christianity has borrowed much from him, but we have modern teachers who are wiser and better adapted to our times than any of the old heathen philosophers.

By the "vision of God," I suppose you mean God in the person of Jesus Christ, for surely you do not expect to see God the Father or God the Holy Ghost. Waiving the question whether the Jesus described in the Gospels was not a phantom, as some of the earliest Christian sects held, or a myth, as there is strong reason to believe others regarded him, I have not a doubt that, if you ever see him in the spirit-world, you will find him to have been a mere man, and by no means a perfect one. Theodore Parker, with the most intense admiration of his character, declared it as his belief that greater and better men than Jesus would yet be born. I venture a step further and say that I believe greater and better men have lived and died than your falsely deified Jesus Christ.

Yours in candor and sincerity,
WM. HENRY BURR.

To Wm. Henry Burr, Esq.

DEAR SIR: You cite an English newspaper to show that some priest, with permission of superiors, has published a catechism containing a very foolish notion of hell, which would make its punishment increase by arithmetical progression. I do not know who this priest may be, nor who his superiors may be, nor how high the authority of the said newspaper may be. Having myself suffered somewhat from newspaper reports, and being indebted, as you know, to such reports for the present discussion, I cannot take your citation from the Manchester *Examiner* as good evidence to indicate what Catholic doctrine is. I will, therefore, dwell upon it no further than to say that "The Sight of Hell" is a very strange title for a *catechism*, and that the long and oratorical citations given are not at all in the catechetical form. As to the notion of hell supposed to be taught in this supposed catechism, I never heard of it before, and think it very absurd. Whatever fluctuations there may be in the miseries of a future life, I can neither admit the idea of any essential diminution of the punishment, nor do I know of any warrant for believing that it will be increased. It is a fixed and permanent state.

The Catholic Church has defined very little in regard to this question. It may be as well to tell you what that little is. It is a matter of faith that there is a hell, or, in other words, that punishment awaits the impenitent sinner in a future life. It is also a matter of faith that this punishment will be eternal. This much every Catholic must believe, or cease to be a Catholic. Perhaps, generally speaking, this much is enough to know.

Outside of these definitions various questions may arise, and Catholics may discuss them freely, and hold different opinions, which, though more or less probable, imply no sin on their part against faith. They may raise questions in regard to the locality of hell. They may debate upon the nature of its punishments. They may argue that the fire and the worm, etc., mentioned in the Sacred Scriptures, are to be understood figuratively, as apt similitudes to designate the pains and griefs of a future life. On the contrary, they may, in the free exercise of their judgment, understand them in the material and literal sense. In discussing such questions, men will speak either learnedly or ignorantly, wisely or foolishly, grossly or spiritually, according to their various gifts and dispositions, and the cultivation of their intellects. This freedom leaves room for mistakes into which even scholars and doctors will sometimes fall. In such case, however, each one is answerable for his own mistakes—neither the Church to which he belongs, nor his fellow-Catholics, stand pledged to sustain him in his blunders.

In using this liberty, however, men must be careful not to impugn or bring into peril certain matters belonging to other provinces of Christian doctrine, which are more elementary in their character, and perhaps points of defined faith. For instance, in their zeal to arouse some torpid conscience, they must not forget to guard safely that most sacred of all subjects, the character of God. His justice must be maintained, that men may look up to him with awe as the competent Ruler of the universe, whose laws cannot be violated with impunity. He must be so represented as to command respect. But it is equally necessary to draw his character in such lines of gentle grace and beauty as may win our love.

The Christian's God is a God of love.

Of all the creatures whom he created, not one can be found exiled beyond the circle of his loving care. He loves not only the just, but the wicked also, including lost men and the fallen angels. He cannot love the wicked as such, but he loves them as his creatures. In every work of God his mercy takes part, even in the condemnation of sinners. For although he cannot without offence to the necessary demands of justice do away with all their punishment, yet always he exacts a less penalty than their sins deserve. Thus, even in the case of the damned, he tempers justice with mercy, and makes them as happy as their continued depravity will allow. No trace of exaggeration is discernible in the grateful tribute of David when he sings, "All the ways of the Lord are mercy and truth." I am writing under no impulse of my own fancy, but thoughtfully and carefully. Upon my table lies that golden manual of theologians, the *Summa* of St. Thomas, and I have weighed each

The Doctrine of Hell. 69

line from the open page before me.* In the God my faith presents to me I find no vindictive and merciless spirit, fertile to invent new methods of torture, gathering and unloosing furious demons to add to the natural and necessary consequences of sin. It is a God of unbounded love and infinite compassion, who desires the hap-

---

* *Summa*, i. qu. xx, art. 2. Utrum Deus omnia amet. See Wisdom xi. 24: "For thou lovest all things that are, and hatest none of the things which thou hast made."

"In damnatione reproborum apparet misericordia, non quidem totaliter relaxans, sed aliqualiter allevians, dum punit citra condignum." *Summa*, i. qu. xxi. art. 4.

For the goodness of God and his *fostering* and *preserving* care extended to all, even to the devils, see Petavius, *De Deo Deique Proprietatibus* l. vi., cap. iii. § vii. "Ea tamen clementer idem et benignè tuetur ac vegetat; quod in dæmonibus, eorumque similibus Adami posteris quotidiè cernimus." See, also S. Aug.: "Non sane creatoris desistente bonitate et malis angelis subministrare vitam, vivacemque potentiam; quae subministratio si auferatur interibunt." *Enchir. ad Laur.* c. xxvii.

piness of all his creatures, and is good even to the thankless and depraved.

Believe me, my friend, he to whose faith and worship I most affectionately call you is no revengeful Jove or Pluto, no unheeding Brahma, no Ogre of the fairy tales to frighten away the loving and confiding heart. He is One in whom infinite majesty is united to boundless and ever-enduring love. You have little esteem for the Bible. Let me quote, then, from a poet who is, or ought to be, by profession a prophet and chorister of nature and of the human heart. We find in his words the great truth which I have just declared, coupled with an excellent lesson of practical piety:

> "He prayeth best who loveth best
> All things both great and small;
> For the dear God that loveth us,
> He made and loveth all."

I believe in a hell, and tremble at the thought of it. But every sad image it brings to my mind only makes me cling more closely to the God I cherish. When my heart throbs with pity for its hapless inmates, I know that it only beats in response to the mightier pulsations of that great Breast on which I lean.

Yours truly,
C. A. WALWORTH.

To the Rev. Clarence Walworth.

DEAR SIR: Your incredulity as to the Catholicity of the doctrine of hell, taught by the Rev. Mr. Furniss, is perhaps justifiable. The Manchester *Examiner*, from which the extracts were taken, is excellent authority, and I have other evidence that the catechism, or whatever else it might be called, was published. But I may possibly have been misled into supposing it was a Catholic book from the use of the expression *permissu superiorum*. Giving you, therefore, the benefit of the doubt, I will endeavor to supply the place of that authority by another to which I am certain you can take no exception. I will advance a "sight of hell" by one of the most noted of the Christian Fathers, Tertullian, who wrote about A.D. 200:

"Yes, and there are other sights: that last day of judgment, with its everlasting issues; that day unlooked for by the nations, the theme of their derision, when the world, hoary with age and all its many products, shall be consumed in one great flame! How vast a spectacle then bursts upon the eye! What there excites my admiration? what my derision? Which sight gives me joy? which rouses me to exultation? As I see so many illustrious monarchs, whose reception into the heavens [as gods] was publicly announced, groaning now in the lowest darkness with great Jove himself, and those, too, who bore witness of their exaltation; governors of provinces, too, who persecuted the Christian name, [burning] in fires more fierce than those with which in the days of their pride they raged against the followers of Christ! That world's wise men besides, the very philosophers, in fact, who taught their followers that God had no concern in aught that is sublunary, and were wont to assure them that either they had no souls, or that they would never return to the bodies which at death they had left, now covered with shame before these poor deluded ones, as one fire consumes them! Poets also trembling, not before the judgment-seat of Rhadamanthus or Minos, but of the unexpected Christ! I shall have a better opportunity then of hearing the tragedians, louder voiced in their own calamity; of viewing play-actors, much more 'dissolute' in the dissolving flame; of looking upon the charioteer, all glowing in his chariot of fire; of witnessing the wrestlers, not in their gymnasia, but tossing in the fiery billows; unless even then I shall not care to attend to such ministers of sin in my eager wish rather to fix a gaze insatiative on those whose fury vented itself against the Lord. . . What quæstor or priest in his munificence will bestow on you the favor of seeing and exulting in such things as these? And yet even now we in a measure have them by faith in the picturings of imagination."—Vol. I. *De Spectaculis*, Ante-Nicene Lib. vol. xi.

The exultation of this eminent Christian saint over the expected final doom of his fellow-creatures who rejected his theology, is paralleled by the pious doggerel of Wigglesworth—

> "The saints behold with courage bold
> and thankful wonderment,
> To see all those that were their foes
> now brought to punishment."

How can you, my friend, persuade yourself that such a being as Knapp, Wigglesworth, Furniss, and Tertullian have described is a God of love? How can you love a God who, for finite offences, inflicts infinite punishment? I am sick of the continual cant about "a God of unbounded love and infinite compassion." I am disgusted with the sentimental poetry of those half-fledged infidels, the Unitarians, ringing changes on "the dear God that loveth us." I arraign and impeach the Jewish poet David when he says, "All the ways of the Lord are mercy and truth." It is inconsistent with what he says elsewhere : " God is angry every day " (Ps. vii. 11)—" Blessed be the Lord, my strength, which teacheth my hands to war and my fingers to fight" (cxliv. 1). See what a character your Holy Bible gives of your God :

I am a jealous God, visiting the iniquity of the fathers upon the children. (Ex. xx. 5.) I make peace and create evil. (Is. xiv. 7.) I frame evil and device against you. (Jer. xviii. 11.) The Lord hath put a lying spirit in the mouth of all these thy prophets. (1 Kings xxii. 23.) If the prophet be deceived when he hath spoken a thing, I the Lord have deceived that prophet. (Ezek. xiv. 9.) God shall send them strong delusion, that they should believe a lie. (2 Thess. ii. 11.) Now go and smite Amalek, and utterly destroy all that they have, and spare them not, but slay both man and woman, infant and suckling. (1 Sam. xv. 2, 3.) For ye have kindled a fire in mine anger which shall burn for ever. (Jer. xvii. 4.)

How painfully you struggle and strain your faith to believe in the justice of the Christian's God! You are now suffering in a degree the torments of the hell that your Church has created; hence that wail of sadness and terror in your closing words—"I believe in a hell, and tremble at the thought of it. . . . My heart throbs with pity for its hapless inmates." Poor child of the Church! I pity you, for I once believed in a hell, and felt the same discomfort you now feel. When I was a Christian, I spoke as a Christian, I understood as a Christian, I thought as a Christian; but when I became a Freethinker, I put away childish, Christian things. Rise up and shake off the nightmare of authority. Obey the voice of reason. Consider that the Church has a mercenary interest in maintaining its dogmas. It will give you a pang to break away from present moorings, but you will embark on serener waters, and will find a more delightful haven of rest for your soul.

WM. HENRY BURR.

To Wm. Henry Burr, Esq.

DEAR SIR: What have I, or what has the doctrine of hell, to do with any cruel spirit that you find, or think you find, in Tertullian? You are mistaken when you call him an eminent Christian saint. He was a heretic, and died in his heresy. But were he otherwise, what force could the extract have in our argument? I am willing to admit that many authors—Catholic authors, too—and more than you know of, have written more objectionable things than anything I find in your quotation from Tertullian. If you can frame any argument upon this admission, do it, and put it in some logical form.

It is wasting words to ask me how "such a being as Knapp, Wigglesworth, etc., have described, is a God of love?" I have told you over and over again that I do not derive my conceptions of God, or of any other doctrine, from these men. It is also wasting words to ask me, "How can I love a God who for finite offences inflicts infinite punishment?" I have said nothing about infinite punishment; it is a difficulty of your own making.

You throw up to me eight distinct passages of Scripture without any note or comment on them of your own. I may be able to conceive, in some sort, what ideas you attach to them, and what kind of argument you might construct on those ideas, but this is not my business. Your part in this discussion is something else than to gather raw and undigested passages from your miscellaneous readings of the Bible, the Fathers, the newspapers, and old psalm-books, and lay them before me for examination and comment. You hold no doctrines of your own in religion, so far as yet appears. You are the attacking party, and have nothing in return to defend. Give me, then, at least the single privilege of a defined, developed, and logical argument to defend against, and spare me this miscellaneous shower of uncommented quotations. Waiting for this, and for want of something better, I revert to your letter of July 16. In that you say: "By the vision of God, I suppose you mean God in the person of Jesus Christ, for surely you do not expect to see God the Father or God the Holy Ghost." Indeed, you are mistaken. The faithful Catholic expects to see in heaven Jesus Christ, not only in his humanity, but in the greatness of his divinity, with the Father and the Holy Ghost. There we shall see God. The reward we look to is nothing less than God himself. "*Ego merces tua magna nimis.*" There he will appear to us, no longer reflected merely in his creation, but as he is in himself. We shall see him as he sees himself; not, indeed, with an equal power of vision, for that power in him is infinite, but by the same mode of vision, namely, by direct view, with no veil interposed between us and the divine essence that we shall look upon.

I grant you that God is not visible to the corporeal eye. In this sense, no man hath seen God at any time. Nor is he directly visible to the mind's eye by any natural faculty of mental vision. It is only by a special gift, a supernatural light, that we can thus behold him, namely, by that same "*lumen gloriæ*" by which the angels look upon his face. Infidels discuss everything from a purely natural point of view, and that view is limited by the dimensions of the world they live in. All of God's creation, matter and spirit, and God himself, must be made to lie within the reach of their eyes and telescopes. The power of God is bounded by the limits of their own horizon, and therefore grace and every supernatural endowment for this life and the other are set aside as impossible. You may hold this for your own philosophy if you like, and

The Doctrine of Hell. 83

you may use it to refute the Christian religion, if you can; but you misrepresent us when you attempt to explain Christian doctrine by it, for that doctrine confederates with a higher philosophy.

"Personally," you say, " I would prefer your hell for infants and idiots to your heaven for saints; for I fear that I should get prodigiously tired of the everlasting vision of God." Alas! my friend, either you have spoken hastily, or else your conception of God is a very feeble one. (I am presuming that you believe in one.) Tired! What is there in him to tire you? If the material universe, together with the whole world of spirits, were laid open to your inspection, would this be a tiresome privilege? If all the glory of the sidereal heavens, all those wondrous revelations which the astronomer searches after with such insatiable eagerness; all those which lie in the air, in the ocean, and under ground; all that beauty which is spread over this world of nature, over the waves, the forests, the hills and valleys, together with that vast under-world of beauty which the philosopher and poet find beneath the surface—if all this were given to you for a pleasure-garden, with the key to every secret in your hand, would you soon grow tired? I do not know your tastes, but I love nature dearly, and I can well understand that joy which the true naturalist feels in exploring this beautiful book of nature, where every leaf he turns is a new revelation of light and beauty.

> "Thou canst not wave thy staff in air,
>   Or dip thy paddle in the lake,
> But it carves the bow of beauty there,
>   And the ripples in rhymes the oar forsake."

Ah! what is all this exhibition of intricacy and order, of unity and variety, of majesty and delicacy, of liberty and harmony, of light and shadow, of beauty ancient and ever new, compared with that infinite variety, that exhaustless wealth of light, life, and beauty, to be found in him who made it all, and of whose radiance it is only at best a dim reflection?

> " He is the axis of the star ;
> He is the sparkle of the spar ;
> He is the heart of every creature :
> He is the meaning of each feature ;
> And his mind is the sky,
> Than all it holds more deep, more high."

What is there in the vision of God that should make you grow tired? It is not an everlasting gaze at some object which can be comprehended at a single glance. Such a conception belongs to the philosophy of a child. It is a new and glorious faculty of vision, by which you would be able to see with the eyes of angels, no longer feebly tracing the footprints of God in the creation, but clearly beholding the Creator himself, and also the creation as it lies mapped in that Creator's mind.

What is joy but to look on that which we love, and know it to be ours? In the possession of God, therefore, the heart and mind both find their supreme bliss. They have all they need and all they can crave. When the one is fed with the highest truth, and the other embraces the highest good, and these are ensured to them for ever, then indeed happiness is supreme, and the restless soul of man can ask no more.

This vision of God is man's original destiny. To lose it is that *pœna damni* which constitutes hell. It is not, indeed, the whole of hell, as I have already stated; but it is the essential and constituent idea of that world of lost souls. Since, then, even unbaptized infants, although free from positive suffering, yet endure this immeasurable loss, it is only by a total misconception of the Christian doctrine that any one can sincerely say, "I prefer the hell of infants and idiots to the heaven of saints." To my mind, nothing can be more mournful and forlorn than the thought of a lost destiny.

Yours truly,
C. A. WALWORTH.

To the Rev. Clarence A. Walworth.

DEAR SIR: The authority of Tertullian as an eminent Christian saint and father of the Church, cannot be evaded by you as a Catholic. He was a presbyter of the Catholic Church, and was regarded by Eusebius, the father of church history, as one of the ablest Latin writers. He employed his great learning vigorously in the cause of Christianity and against heathens and heretics; and though toward the latter part of his life he quitted the Orthodox Church and adhered to the Montanist sect, for which heresy his name has not been transmitted to us with the title of saint (Biog. Dic.), yet the ground of his separation related rather to discipline than doctrine (Enc. Am.), and the difference between his writings before and after he became a Montanist is more of spirit than of doctrine, so that they are classed in authority with those of the other Church fathers (Am. Cyc.) But I do not rest the case here. I aver that Tertullian's conception of hell was not only the orthodox doctrine of the Church of his time, but that it was maintained with augmented horrors up to and even after the Reformation, as one of the most essential dogmas of the Catholic Church. Lecky, in his *History of Rationalism* (vol. iii., p. 341, and following), says:

"It would be difficult, and perhaps not altogether desirable, to attain in the present day to any realized conception of the doctrine of future punishment as it was taught by the early fathers, and elaborated and developed by the mediæval priests. That doctrine has now been thrown so much into the background, it has been so modified and softened and explained away, that it scarcely retains a shadow of its ancient repulsiveness. . . Perhaps the most acute pain the human body can undergo is that of fire; and this the early fathers assure us is the eternal destiny of the mass of mankind. The doctrine was stated with the utmost literalism and precision. In the two first Apologies for the Christian faith, it was distinctly asserted. . . Origen, it is true, and his disciple, Gregory of Nyssa, in a somewhat hesitating manner, diverged from the prevailing opinion, and strongly inclined to a figurative interpretation, and to a belief in the ultimate salvation of all; but they were alone in their opinion. With these two exceptions, all the fathers proclaim the eternity of torments, and all define these torments as the action of a literal fire upon a sensitive body. When the Pagans argued that the body could not remain for ever unconsumed in a material flame, they were answered by the analogies of the salamander, the asbestus, and the volcano, and by appeals to the Divine Omnipotence, which was supposed to be

The Doctrine of Hell. 91

continually exerted to prolong the tortures of the dead."

"After the religious terrorism that followed the twelfth century, that doctrine attained its full elaboration. The agonies of hell seemed then the central fact of religion and the perpetual subject of the thoughts of men. All literature, all painting, all eloquence was concentrated upon the same dreadful theme. By the pen of Dante, by the pencil of Orgagna, by the pictures that crowded every church and the sermons that rang from every pulpit, the maddening terror was sustained. The saint was even permitted in vision to behold the agonies of the lost, and to recount the spectacle he had witnessed. He loved to tell how by the lurid glare of the eternal flames he had seen millions writhing in every form of ghastly suffering, their eye-balls rolling with unspeakable anguish, their limbs gashed, mutilated, and quivering with pain, tortured by pangs that seemed ever keener by the recurrence, and shrieking in vain for mercy to an unpitying heaven."

Again, in his *History of European Morals* (vol. ii., p. 335, and following), he speaks of the custom of Catholic priests of imprinting upon the minds of young children ghastly and atrocious pictures of future misery, and adds this note:

"Few Englishmen, I imagine, are aware of the infamous publications written with this object that are circulated by the Catholic priests among the poor. I have before me a tract 'for children and young persons,' called *The Sight of Hell*, by the Rev. J. Furniss, C.SS.R., published '*permissu superiorum*' by Duffy (Dublin and London). It is a detailed description of the dungeons of hell, and a few sentences may serve as a sample."

After describing the torments of a girl about sixteen years old standing with

The Doctrine of Hell. 93

bare feet on a red-hot floor, and of a boy in a boiling kettle, the fifth dungeon is described, and the citation concludes as follows:

"The little child is in this red-hot oven. Hear how it screams to come out. See how it turns and twists itself about in the fire. It beats its head against the roof of the oven. It stamps its little feet on the floor. . . . God was very good to this child. Very likely God saw it would get worse and worse and never repent, and so it would have to be punished much more in hell. So God in his mercy called it out of the world in its early childhood."

I thank the unknown correspondent of the *Investigator* for enabling me to verify the above as Catholic authority. Knapp was a true representative of modern evangelical Christianity, Wigglesworth of New England Puritanism, Tertullian of primitive Catholicism, and Furniss of its more modern phase. You admit the "cruel spirit" of Tertullian's conception, and the "foolish notion of hell" entertained by Furniss. You ask me to "frame an argument upon this admission, and put it in some logical form." Pray, what need of any argument on my part?

You say you "have said nothing about infinite punishment." Indeed! Is not eternal punishment infinite in duration?

You complain of my citing passages of Scripture without comment. Are they not in your estimation a part of God's revelation? If, then, I forbear to comment on them, should not their meaning be plain enough? Have I garbled any passage? It is a pitiful Word of God that needs a commentator. You have quoted from the Bible and from divers poets (once, I believe, from a Unitarian hymn-book), and have referred approvingly to certain authorities of the Church. I, in turn, have quoted from the Scriptures, from the Puritan poet Wigglesworth, and from certain other authorities of the Church. But lo! you tell me that my part in this discussion is "something else than to gather raw and undigested passages from [my] miscellaneous readings of the Bible, the fathers, the newspapers, and old psalm-books, and lay them before [you] for examination"; and you call upon me to give you some logical argument to defend against, and to spare you "this miscellaneous shower of uncommented quotations." Again I say, what need of argument on my part? The hideousness of the dogmas is enough. I present them in all their naked ugliness as the best argument against the Christian Church, whether Catholic or Protestant. As regards "raw and undigested passages," the Bible is full of them. I once tried to digest them, and imagined they were spiritual food, but at length they turned my stomach and I puked them up.

The natural point of view is the only

one from which to discuss anything. We know nothing of the supernatural. It is a contradictory term, implying miracle. There may be *preter*natural senses, but we, in our normal state, do not possess them. Convinced as I am, from modern Spiritual phenomena alone, that there is a life beyond, though I can form no conception of its pursuits and duties, I expect in the next world to have a more comprehensive vision of the material and spiritual universe. Of that vision I shall never tire; but as to the "everlasting vision of God," whether in one person or three—whether as an old man, a young man, and a dove (for thus are they pictured to our senses by the Romish Church), or in any other personal shape, I repeat that I should get prodigiously tired of it. If Jesus of Nazareth was not a mere myth, like the Pagan Apollo or Prometheus, I may hope to see him. But so little do I know of his real character and works, that I would rather first seek the acquaintance of those worthy philanthropists of whom I know more, such as Socrates and Plato, Thomas Paine and John Brown.

          Yours truly,
              WM. HENRY BURR.

To Wm. Henry Burr, Esq.

DEAR SIR: I am sorry that you still persist in holding me obligated to defend all that individual Christians have preached or written. I have insisted, and insist again, that as a Catholic Christian I am not responsible for the opinions even of Catholics, however holy their character or high their station, except so far as they agree with the promulgated creeds and solemn definitions of the Catholic Church—a target broad enough for any fair antagonist.* If you are unwilling to meet me upon that platform of faith which I avow; if you dare not maintain your infidel hostility to that holy Church upon her own ground; if you feel driven to be-

---

* The Canons and Decrees of the Council of Trent alone, which are mostly doctrinal, occupy in my edition two hundred and seventy-six pages of a large octavo volume. C. W.

come a scavenger of history, a compiler of all the extravagances published by individual Christians during eighteen centuries, forming out of such material a man of straw of your own creation to cross swords with—why, then, you are only one new instance of that system of loud whooping and timorous skulking which characterizes Indian warfare. It requires but little genius to make large generalizations, and bolster them up by particular instances. Many modern authors do this, and call it the philosophy of history. All crotchets may be justified by history in this manner. In this way Lecky and other infidel theorizers impose their bastard systems on the public. I had hoped to meet you front to front in a manlier strife, and trust it may be so yet.

Since you have explained that by "infinite" punishment for finite offences you mean *endless* punishment, your argument on that head resolves itself into this: that you hold it to be unjust and cruel in God to punish sins that are limited in degree by a penalty that is unlimited in duration. I reply, that since sin in the creature is necessarily limited in the degree of its malice, it is also limited in the degree of its penalty; but since sin unrepented of is perpetual in the heart of the sinner, it is also necessarily perpetual in the duration of its punishment. Thus the proportion between sin and its penalty is maintained throughout.

Your quotations from the Bible afforded you a fair opportunity for argument had your style of controversy allowed you to follow them up. Failing this, and since you will not accept my invitation to do so, I must needs take them in hand, and reply to insinuation where I would have preferred reasoning. I will endeavor to dispose of these passages in such way as may save you the trouble of going over the same ground again, by emptying a bag of similar texts another time.

No book was ever written without the

The Doctrine of Hell.

use of tropes or figures. The Bible abounds with them. Among these we often find metaphorically attributed to God things which, in their literal sense, are utterly inconsistent with his nature. Thus reference is made to his head, hands, feet, reins, to his seeing, speaking, laughing, etc., to express some divine characteristic in popular language. The necessity for this does not lie in the poverty of that divine power from which the revelation proceeds, but in the limited resources of that human intelligence to which the revelation is made. Shall it be inferred from such expressions that God has a body? If so, then when Virgil says "*fama volat*," we must conclude that, in his opinion, rumor is a bird having wings. In the same popular language God is said to be jealous, angry, in a fury, full of vengeance, etc., and, on the contrary, pacified, relenting, and repenting.* Such

---

* In God there is no hatred in the sense of enmity (*odium inimicitiæ*), by which one wishes evil to an-

words are not to be taken in a literal sense. The Bible teaches in the plainest terms that God is a purely spiritual and simple being. As he is without body or parts, so is he without passions; that is, without any sensitive or emotional nature, and incapable, moreover, of anything like irresolution or change of mind. To carp at expressions like the above, which the sacred writers use *humano more* only, is utterly unworthy of a scholar, or of any sincere and intelligent mind.

Using a like liberty, the prophet Isaias represents God as saying, "*I form the*

other for sake of the suffering which it causes him, but only that hatred by which one detests evil as evil (*odium abominationis*). God is not, therefore, in any strict sense of the word, the enemy of any being, and where the language of the Bible, or that of the preacher, seems to assert this, it must be understood in accordance with the principles of sound theology. God is only the enemy of a lost soul in the sense that he must needs, in justice, punish him, and that the complacency and familiar intercourse which constitutes friendship is in such case for ever excluded.

light and create darkness; I make peace and create evil." Of course, neither darkness nor evil are created things, nor have they any real existence at all, darkness being simply the absence of light, as every student of natural science knows, and evil being simply the absence of some good, as every philosopher knows. The true meaning of the above passage is very well given in the *Morals* of St. Gregory: "The Lord is said to create evil, when, out of things well constructed and in their nature good, he forms a whip for those that do evil." (3 Mor. 7.) Even infidels are accustomed to use such expressions as these: "Every sin carries with it its own punishment;" and "The sinner makes his own hell." They thus acknowledge an universal law of retribution for evil-doing. Christians acknowledge this same law, only in our belief no laws are attributed to blind chance. To us they are simply the principles by which God governs the universe.

Now, let us consider that divine order given to Saul to exterminate the Amalekites, and other similar commandments. I do not purpose to make any apology for these things. They are to be considered as acts of government, belonging to the supreme jurisdiction of the Lord and Master of all. It is what the lawyers call the " right of eminent domain," *dominium eminens*. I am not sorry that you have raised this question; for if I have been anxious hitherto to set forth the goodness and infinite love of God for all his creatures, I am equally zealous to assert the rights of his sovereignty. I affirm, therefore, that God is not only your Creator and Redeemer, but that he is also your Master. It is he who gave you your life, and he has the right to take it away. He gave it without asking your permission, and he has the right to take it away when he pleases. He may take it away as an act of punishment, or he may take it away as an act of mercy, or he may take it for other reasons, in which reasons your own merits or demerits may have little part. He may take it by means of sickness, or by some more sudden visitation of his providence. He may take it by the condemnation and sentence of a jury and a judge, or by the hand of a soldier in battle. In such case, too, it is equally his doing. From God alone the judge derives his authority to condemn you, and the soldier in battle his right to kill you. Should your life be taken by an assassin, the assassin has no authority from God, but yet God permits it to be done; and if, while condemning the deed, he does not arrest the blow, it is because your death may serve wise purposes of his own. A strange God, indeed, would he be if his prerogatives did not reach as far as all this.

By the right of eminent domain a state may take away the property of any of its subjects for necessary public uses. The dominion of God is still clearer in its title, and more far-reaching in its extent. By it the destruction of the Amalekite nation is fully justified. I might easily dwell upon the former aggressions of this nation against the chosen people of God; their continued and actual hostility; their threatening position upon the flank of the Hebrew territory; the idolatrous and corrupt character of their religion, and the danger of corruption which would ensue should their women and children be spared to mingle with their conquerors. This, however, would only be advancing such reasons of human policy as suggest themselves to my feeble intelligence, and would undoubtedly come far short of the entire array of motives which urged the Divine Ruler of Israel when he gave his severe commandment to Samuel and to Saul. I place my justification of this and other similar acts on higher ground. I place it on that sovereign dominion, reaching to life and death, which vests in God as Creator and absolute Ruler of the world.

He is accustomed to give life when he will, and to recall it when he pleases, from the young and from the old, from the innocent and from the guilty. As with individuals, so with the masses. We see nations increase and prosper; we see races become extinct; and in all this we recognize the hand of God. Rarely, if ever, can we pronounce upon the special motives which guide him in this his administration of life and death. One thing we Christians know well, that God's purposes in the government of mankind reach further than human policy; that they look forward mainly beyond the grave; and that

> "'Tis not the whole of life to live,
> Nor all of death to die."

Lift your own thoughts higher, my friend. Your nature is nobler, and your destiny (if you reach it) higher, than you have been accustomed of late to think.

Yours truly,

C. A. WALWORTH.

To the Rev. Clarence A. Walworth.

DEAR SIR: I hoped you would have continued the discussion in the same courteous spirit with which it began; but in your last letter you more than intimate that I am "only one new instance of the loud whooping and timorous skulking which characterizes Indian warfare." I appeal to every reader if I have not met every question fairly and squarely. But even if you think otherwise, would not courtesy forbid and prudence avoid the use of such expressions as the above, leaving the argument to rest upon its merits? It would doubtless suit you better to confine me to "the promulgated creeds" of the Catholic Church, which you think afford "a target broad enough for any fair antagonist," but I choose to assail opinions that have been or are now held by the authority or consent of the Church, whether expressed in written creeds or otherwise. And it is not, as you would have it appear, "a man of straw" that I create and assail; it is not exceptional individual extravagances that I display, but unanimously approved doctrines. Little may be found in Catholic creeds about endless torment, but I have proved that it has been a most awfully prominent doctrine of your Church. Infant damnation is not clearly taught in the Presbyterian creed, and yet the preacher who would have dared two hundred years ago to question it publicly would have been branded as a heretic. But show me to-day the Protestant parson or layman that dare avow his belief in that horrid dogma. So with the Catholic Inquisition; its specific approval may not be found in any of the "solemn definitions of the Church," but it was a Church institution nevertheless, and woe to the priest who protested against it.

I take no offence at being called "a scavenger of history" for the purpose of exposing the filth that your Church seeks to hide from the light of the nineteenth century. But since you claim that I have made no argument upon the facts, I will now submit an argument in the words of that "infidel theorizer" whom you politely charge with imposing a "bastard system" of so-called "philosophy of history" upon the public. After portraying the awful conceptions of future punishment entertained by the Church in the Middle Ages, Lecky thus speaks of the tendency of such a belief:

"There can be little question that, in the vast majority of cases, its tendency will be to indurate the character, to diffuse abroad a callousness to the sufferings of others that will profoundly debase humanity. If you make the detailed and exquisite torments of multitudes the habitual object of the thoughts and imaginations of men, you will necessarily produce in most of them a gradual indifference to human suffering, and in some of them a disposition to regard it with positive delight. If you further assure men that sufferings form an integral part of a revelation which they are bound to regard as a message of good tidings, you will induce them to stifle every feeling of pity, and almost encourage their insensibility to virtue. . . . When the doctrine was intensely realized or implicitly believed, it must, therefore, have had one or other of two effects—it must have produced an intensity of compassion that would involve extreme unhappiness and would stimulate to extreme heroism, or it would have produced an absolute callousness and a positive inclination to inflict suffering upon the heretic. It does not require much knowledge of human nature to perceive that the spirit of Torquemada must be more common than that of Xavier."—*History of Rationalism*, vol. i. p. 354.

Not satisfied with the presentation of facts which I thought needed no comment, you ask me to meet you in a "manlier strife." Well, there is my argument; if it is not a fair, square, and manly one, then I am too obtuse to know what is.

"To punish sins that are limited in degree by a penalty that is endless in duration" (I quote your own words), is a doctrine so shocking to human nature that it needs only to be stated to be hated. A God who would punish thus is a fiend. The fallacy of your logic is in the assumption that a finite offence is repeated *ad infinitum*. So, then, I reassert, your doctrine is that, for a finite offence, man suffers infinite punishment.

Your attempt to dispose of the Scripture texts that I collated is ridiculously absurd. I may well forbear "emptying a bag of similar texts another time," because the first one has smothered you. Beginning with the false assumption that none of the expressions in regard to God's body, his seeing, hearing, speaking, repenting, being jealous, angry, etc., are to be understood in a literal sense, you assert what is likewise a mistake—that the Bible teaches that God is "a purely spiritual and simple being," without body or parts, without passions or emotions, incapable, therefore, of "irresolution or change of mind."* Indeed! A God incapable of love or pity! Be careful, my friend, or you will find him to be not different from the God of the atheist—*i.e.* no God at all. I am at a loss to conceive what kind of a Being you hope to meet in the next world; and, when you say you expect to meet three of your Gods in one, I give it up. It is one of those profound mysteries, I suppose, that are "revealed (only) unto babes."

* Mr. Burr does not seem to understand that pure love is an inclination of the pure and simple will, and therefore wholly spiritual; whereas, emotional or passional love has either its origin, or that quality which makes it emotional, in our sensitive animal nature, and cannot therefore be attributed to God, who is a pure spirit.

But the God who forms the light and makes peace you say cannot create darkness nor evil, as the Bible says he does, because those are negative things, without " any real existence." So when God is said to blind the eyes and harden the hearts of his creatures, lest they should be converted, I suppose it is to be understood in a negative way—that is, that he does not do any such thing, and that blindness and obduracy have no real existence!

Finally, you strive to justify the extermination of the Amalekites by the "right of eminent domain," and the further right of a soldier to kill his enemy in battle. By the first, you assert that " a state may take away the property of any of its subjects for necessary uses." I deny it. As stated, it is not a legal maxim, but a self-evident falsehood. The common law requires that, in taking the property of a citizen for public uses, due compensation shall be awarded. The same rule applies to the possessions of an alien, and of another nation or people. The alleged right of the soldier to kill his enemy in battle is also another self-evident falsehood. His enemy has just the same right to kill him, and no more. It is force struggling against force, and the strongest wins, right or wrong.

But when you seek to apply these false principles to the Jewish people, you make sad work. You first set forth the goodness and infinite love of your God (who is "without passions"), and then you represent him as an arbitrary Master, who stands quietly by and permits assassins to kill their fellow-men, women, and children, all for presumptively wise purposes! This is the old theological sophistry which has wrought such horrors all over Christendom. Falsely assuming that God ordered the Israelites to exterminate the heathen, the bloody Cortez and his successors went forth under the banner of the cross, and slew the innocent inhabitants of America by the hundred thousand. So, also, the New England Puritans, imagining themselves a chosen people like the Jews, and having resolved, first, "That the earth belongs to the saints," and, secondly, "That we are the saints," proceeded to rob the aboriginal inhabitants of this country of their lands, and to take their lives when they resisted. What though an ancient anonymous writer says God commanded wholesale robbery and murder! The heart of humanity revolts at it as a libel on God Almighty. The Pentateuch is as full of falsehoods as a cullender is full of holes. Bishop Colenso has proved this from internal evidence so plain that a child can understand it. Like the Book of Mormon, the Pentateuch, together with most of the other Books of the Bible, is a transparent fraud. And yet the writers of it may have been as innocent of fraudulent intent as was the Rev. Samuel Spalding, who wrote the Book of Mormon. It is the Jewish and

Christian hierarchies that have imposed the false and immoral Books of the Bible upon the people as the inspired Word of God.

Do not deceive yourself, my friend, by presuming that the readers of the *Investigator* are ignorant of theology. Very many of them have made it the study of their lives. I claim to be among that number. After long and arduous study, I am convinced that theology is built upon assumption alone, and that those who think they know something about it in fact know nothing. Whether you can make much headway in discussing the subject with such an antagonist as I, and before such a tribunal as the readers of the *Investigator*, is for you to consider. I am glad to have elicited the discussion thus far, and am willing to continue it as long as you and the editor of the paper deem it expedient.

Yours truly,
WM. HENRY BURR.

To Wm. Henry Burr, Esq.

DEAR SIR: I beg leave to invite your attention to the special ground in dispute between us, and to the very strange manner in which you have endeavored to force upon me a platform of your own making. In the beginning, instead of stating your objections to the *Catholic* doctrine, you presented representations of hell drawn by Elder Knapp and certain Puritan clergymen of New England. I replied that this would not do in discussion with me, a Roman Catholic; that the doctrines which I accept are those defined by the Catholic Church.

B. Well, then, look at this picture of hell given by a priest named Furniss!

W. I do not know who the priest may be. I think his notions very absurd. They make no part of Catholic faith; and, to save you further trouble, I state distinctly what the Catholic faith is on this subject. The Church has defined that there is a hell, and that its punishment is everlasting. This much every Catholic must believe. The Church has made no further definitions. Outside of this, each Catholic is free to use his own opinion. He is also answerable for his own blunders.

B. But now look at this picture by Tertullian, a Father, and an eminent Christian saint! He actually seems to exult over the doom of his fellow-creatures.

W. What has the exulting of Tertullian to do with the truth of the doctrine of hell? Besides, he was no saint. I am here to sustain the Church's faith. She has spoken for herself.

B. Now, do accept my view of hell, so that I may attack it conveniently after the usual fashion. And really it is the Orthodox doctrine, and one of the most essential dogmas of the Catholic Church. Hear what Lecky says.

W. Lecky's statements are nothing to me. He is himself an infidel, writing in the interests of the infidel cause, and as improper a person as yourself to lay down a platform for a Catholic Christian. Take the Church's faith as she herself defines it. Bring me arguments, and cease furnishing me with platforms.

B. Indeed, you are very unreasonable. But since you will have it so, I bring you now an argument which I can recommend as a fair, square, and manly one. After portraying the awful conceptions of future punishment entertained (as he says) by the Church in the Middle Ages, Lecky thus argues upon the tendency of *such* a belief to indurate the character of men, and "produce in most of them a gradual indifference to human suffering, and in some of them a disposition to regard it with positive delight," etc., etc.

Now, friend Burr, in order that this argument may be a fair and square one, I shall take it for granted that (in your own intention, at least) it is levelled against such " awful conceptions " of hell *only* as attach to the Church's avowed doctrine, and as are *necessarily* contained in the words of our Saviour, who calls it an undying worm and an unquenchable fire. I have never wished to deny—I feel the fact most solemnly—that to the impenitent sinner these words (whether literally or figuratively true) are awful. On the other hand, I not only admit, but maintain, that it is possible to dwell upon this subject too much ; and that, especially when dwelt upon with great detail of imagination, and a cold-blooded dissection of sensitive nerves, it becomes revolting and mischievous. But the same principle applies to all punishments. The penalty of death for murder I hold to be most just and necessary ; but I am always sorry to have these scenes of execution paraded before the public eye with all its harassing details of leave-taking, speech-making, ostentatious praying, dangling upon the rope, etc., nor do I like to read of them. The death of the criminal is awful enough in its naked truth. If Lecky's argument and yours goes no further than this, I can clasp hands with you most heartily.

If, however, you mean to insist that no punishment shall take place; that the penalty in itself is immoral in its tendency, as well as the needless or excessive display of it, your argument is simply ridiculous. Such a principle would not only do away with hell, but with all capital punishment, with the prison-cell, and with our whole code of criminal justice. Even the naughty little children would go unwhipped, and the ferule would be banished from house and schoolhouse, for fear that it " might produce in them a gradual indifference to human suffering, and in some of them a disposition to regard it with positive delight." This objection will not do, Brother Burr. Try again; and, if I may presume to counsel, try without Lecky. He is a Jack-o' lantern at best, and can only lead you into the bog.

I myself, however, cannot allow Mr. Lecky to go without a parting word to show how utterly unworthy of confidence his assertions are. Turn, for instance, to your first quotation from him in a previous letter. It is not true, as he states, that, with the exception of Origen and St. Gregory of Nyssa, all the Fathers defined the torments of hell as the action of a *literal* fire upon a sensitive body. Among those who held to a figurative sense are to be numbered, not only St. Gregory of Nyssa, but also St. Ambrose and St. John of Damascus, and (unless we accept an amendment of the text, as some insist) St. Gregory the Great. St. Jerome gives it as the opinion of many in his day, while St. Augustine varied in judgment, both opinions being found in different works. Calmet mentions both opinions as held by many doctors on either side. (Comment on Mark ix. 43; also both

Calmet and Corn. a Lapide on Eccl. vii. 19.) I do not cite these Fathers to advance any opinion of my own. My private *opinions* (which you will please to distinguish from my *faith*) are of little consequence in this discussion. I only wish to show how unreliable Lecky is in his sweeping generalizations. And even in those cases where the facts stated or insinuated by him are not absolutely untrue, he is still unreliable. He possesses a faculty which an admirer of the historian Froude calls " the power of assimilating all facts to the theory established in his own mind," which I take to be, in plain words, the facility of systematically lying for special purposes. As for Lecky's highly colored picture of what he calls the " religious terrorism that followed the twelfth century." I must simply say that, even were it all true (which I deny), it could not be made available to fasten any exaggerated doctrine upon the Church. Catholics are not accustomed to resort to orators, poets, painters, or private visions and revelations for the accurate determination of Christian doctrine. Their truth and accuracy are tested by theology. Theology is not tested by them.

You misrepresent my argument in regard to the justice of an endless punishment. That argument amounts to this: that so long as the same wicked will which prompted the offence remains unchanged, so long sin remains in possession of the heart, and pardon is impossible. In the same loose sense in which you call the punishment infinite (namely, that it goes on without ever ceasing), in that very same sense the sin is infinite. The true location of sin is in the heart or will. Man sees only the outward action, and judges that. God sees the heart, and judges that. Sin is not merely a transitory external act: it is also a habit or continuing attitude of the soul. A hardened heart is permanent alienation from

God; and, since God is the source of all good, permanent alienation from him supposes hopeless misery. *A final, changeless state of alienation from God is hell.* Can you understand this? And can you answer it without again resorting to misrepresentation? Try.

Yours truly,

C. A. WALWORTH.

To the Rev. Clarence A. Walworth.

DEAR SIR: In regard to the question of future punishment which you invited me to discuss, you admit that the Catholic Church " has defined very little"; and yet you insist that I shall be restricted to its " promulgated creeds " and " solemn definitions." I, on the contrary, insist that it is both right and proper for me to prove, as I have done, what notions of hell have been generally, if not unanimously, taught by your Church, and to hold it responsible for the logical consequences of such teaching. In spite of all your efforts, you cannot wipe out the " damned spot " of a hell of literal fire and torments the most intolerable as the generally accepted dogma of what you call " the only Church of Christ on earth." In vain you try to shake off the authority of Tertullian and Furniss; and in vain you seek to impeach Lecky, calling him an "infidel theorizer" and a "Jack-o'-lantern," and accusing him of lying. Apply the test of veracity to your ancient Church authorities, and how many of them would survive the ordeal? Certain it is that some of the most eminent of them confessed themselves liars, and defended lying for the sake of aiding the cause on which their livelihood depended. Can you say as much of "infidel theorizers?" What one of them can be justly suspected of being influenced by mercenary motives? What one had anything to gain by falsehood? Is there no moral courage or self-sacrifice required, on the other hand, to oppose a popular religious belief? How much more to oppose all creeds, and bring down upon one's head both Papal and Protestant authorities!

Thomas Paine prudently postponed his theological essay until his political work was accomplished, and the guillotine warned him to hasten and write his long-

The Doctrine of Hell. 129

contemplated "Age of Reason." What if Lecky chanced to overlook two or even three among the late Fathers who inclined to the milder and figurative notion of Origen in regard to future torments, can you shake Lecky's proofs as to the unanimity of the belief of the early Church in a hell of literal fire? But even if you could prove that your authorities were divided, how much milder would the dogma appear? Even the Presbyterians in 1648, who certainly never augmented the gloom of any doctrine they inherited from the Catholic Church, inserted in their catechism a description of the punishment in the world to come in these words: "Most grievous torments in soul and *body*, without intermission in hell-fire for ever." Is it to be supposed that the Catholic Church of that period entertained or taught any milder notion? Did not your own venerable father, Chancellor Walworth, as a devout Presbyterian, adhere to that solemn definition of his

Church? Even in my young days, to doubt the doctrine of a literal hell-fire was to be in danger of Universalism.

Conceding the force of Lecky's argument as to the immoral tendency of the doctrine of hell, such as he describes it, you claim that, in order to be fair, the argument should be levelled against the conception of future punishment contained in the words of Jesus, who, you say, calls it "an undying worm and an unquenchable fire." The expression referred to is found only in Mark, who has borrowed it from Isaiah lxvi. 24, where it applies to dead carcasses of men, which were to be "an abhorring unto all flesh." Certainly Isaiah never meant by the figure of speech, "their worm shall not die, neither shall their fire be quenched," to teach the doctrine of endless misery, for up to his time there is not the slightest intimation in the Old Testament that the Jews believed even in immortality. How absurd, therefore, to infer the doctrine of endless

The Doctrine of Hell. 131

misery from a repetition of that passage put into the mouth of Jesus by the writer of the Gospel according to Mark! But aside from the meaning of the figure, you have first to prove that the Book of Mark is authentic, true, and inspired, none of which you can do. So, then, I deny that Jesus ever taught the doctrine of an endless hell; but if he did, I hesitate not to say it was an immoral doctrine.

Your reasoning by analogy in regard to the justice of eternal punishment, by comparing it to our " code of criminal justice," and especially to the infliction of capital punishment, is as unfortunate as your prior argument based upon the unqualified right of eminent domain and of a soldier to kill his enemy. I answer the one as I did the other—by denying the right of society to kill anybody, or even to imprison anybody *as a punishment*. Humanity revolts against the death penalty, and is beginning to abrogate it, while by steady steps it is coming to realize that the duty of society is *reformation* and not punishment. Even the whip and the ferule, which you think a necessity, are banished from many a school-house with most excellent results, and parents are learning that sparing the rod does *not* spoil the child. So as mankind grow wiser, they will eschew the old theological chimera that sin is the fruit of innate depravity ("pure cussedness," in vulgar parlance), and learn to deal gently with the erring, whose frailties are the result of ignorance and want of development.

In order to make out that I have misrepresented your argument as to the justice of endless punishment, you assume that, in a "loose sense," a single sin is infinite—that is, it remains in the heart for ever unless pardoned. A very loose sense indeed!—nothing short of nonsense! It is a bald assumption that sin alienates the creature from his Maker, and an equally bald assumption that God can abate the penalty by pardoning the penitent. I affirm that God can no more forgive sin than he can prevent evil. Both are necessary consequences of an undeveloped condition, and both are undergoing slow elimination by advancing knowledge. I therefore make short work of the doctrine of " endless punishment." Transient suffering must follow the violation of natural law, but wisdom is our saviour.

Perhaps this discussion is becoming tedious to the readers of the *Investigator*. If so, I am willing to close it, and, if possible, to allow you the last word. I am glad to be able to say that the tone of your articles has elicited not only my own approbation, but that of all who have expressed an opinion to me on the subject. In that regard, it is in striking contrast with the temper manifested by a Presbyterian priest of this city, who bullied me into a discussion of the Sabbath question. It seems as if your heart's desire is to embrace in the salvation offered by your Church all mankind. Come up on my platform, my dear brother, and you *can* embrace them all. I belong to the broad church of humanity; you are my fellow-member, and I trust that you will ever show by your good works that you are "in good and regular standing." Amen!

          Yours truly,

                WM. HENRY BURR.

To Wm. Henry Burr, Esq.

DEAR SIR: I do not know whether, as you seem to think, this discussion has become tedious to the readers of the *Investigator*. You say you are willing to close it. So am I. I have only this much more to say, and leave it to yourself whether it shall be that "last word" which you proffer me so courteously.

It is evident from some passages of your letter that you confound the general doctrine of *physical* punishments in hell (*pœna sensus*) with the special idea of a *literal* fire, or heat produced by natural combustion. You seem to suppose that either one must understand the "everlasting fire" spoken of in the Bible literally, or else he must reject all idea of bodily pains. You are mistaken. It is the want of theological and even of logical discipline that leads your mind into these constant misconceptions. Now, for my own part, I have not the least doubt that in hell the punishment of actual sins, whatever it may be, embraces the entire sinner such as it finds him ; and therefore, after the resurrection of the body, extends to that body also. Why should I think otherwise? I believe in the resurrection. I understand that the union of a rational soul with a material body constitutes the integrity or completeness of man's complex nature, and therefore the resurrection of the body is required to restore man to that integrity. I am conscious, also, of that intimate intercommunion and mutual sympathy which must exist between soul and body. So believing and understanding, it would be strange indeed to conceive of a hell of misery for the one, and of enjoyment for the other.

I see nothing else in your letter that calls for an explanation, or that requires any answer.

And now let me call attention to the

ignoble and unmanly position which infidelity holds in this controversy. The great question which always has, always will, always must, occupy the human mind, and fill it with anxiety, is

> "The fate of the man-child,
> The meaning of man."

To settle, in the first place, the grave question of his origin—whence he came, and why he is. And wrapped in one problem with this, and requiring one solution, comes to each one of us that other trembling interrogatory, Whither am I tending? What is my destiny in the future?

The meaning of our life is contained in the answer to these questions. LIFE QUESTIONS are they, therefore, and must be met by every man who puts himself forward among his fellow-men as a preceptor and guide. And how do you meet them? I see advertised and offered for sale publications of yours entitled "Nitro-Glycerine Magazines," which are written in opposition to the Christian solution of these questions, and therefore suppose in their author some superior knowledge of the questions themselves. We have, besides, your own boastful assurance that you have made theology the study of your life. You profess, therefore, to have something to say to the public on these matters. What have you, then, to say to us? What is this life of ours—this narrow isthmus between two oceans—this "confused noise between two silences"? We look back with wonder, and see nothing behind the cradle; we look forward with anxiety, but our eyes cannot penetrate beyond the grave. What has Wm. Henry Burr to say? Will he bring us a light? Wm. Henry Burr has nothing to say. He has no light at present. He says that he is "convinced from modern Spiritual phenomena that there is a life beyond"; but he has no further revelations. The spirits that rap under his table are not communicative. But he says, "I expect in the next world to have a more comprehensive vision." Alas! what a pity that we cannot afford to wait! Our time is precious; it hurries us on so rapidly that we fear our own destinies will be sealed before this vision comes to Wm. Henry Burr. Indeed, when it comes to him, as it undoubtedly will, it may be too late for his own good; nor will he be permitted to come back and tell his tale to us.

What is true of Wm. Henry Burr is true of the entire school of infidel writers to which he belongs. They can throw no light upon these momentous questions. They have none. They pretend to none. They have not even a philosophy of the future state. Cynics and mockers merely, they have nothing to say in regard to these matters, except, like Diogenes, to sit in their tubs, and rail at those who have something to say. Know-nothings by profession, they glory in their ignorance. It is strange that, in these great questions of life and death and destiny, there should be found any souls simple enough to take counsel from professed ignorants, to seek light from those who acknowledge themselves to be in the dark. If an infidel catechism were written, it would necessarily be something like this:

Q.—Who made you?
A.—I don't know.
Q.—Did any one make you?
A.—I don't know.
Q.—What is the cause of your being?
A.—I don't know.
Q.—What is the underlying principle of your life, by force of which you still continue to live?
A.—I don't know.
Q.—Will you be accountable to any one after death for the manner in which you spend your life?
A.—I don't know.
Q.—Good child! Now repeat the infidel's prayer.
A.—O God! if there be any God, have

The Doctrine of Hell. 141

mercy on my soul if I have any soul, when I die, if there be anything left of me after my death. Amen!

If infidel authors have no light to throw upon the gloom of the future, they have plenty of water to throw upon the light. Their philosophy is not constructive; its efficacy lies in destruction. If they cannot teach us anything, they will be happy to show us that there is nothing to be learned. They cannot build, but they are practised in the art of undermining. They have no respect for a beaver-dam, but they will bow down profoundly to a rat-hole.

Out upon this "nitro-glycerine" literature! Away with this philosophy of scepticism, this science of negation, this destruction in lieu of edification, this vision of the mole, this progress of the crab! Like dogs in the manger, some souls can take no food nor suffer others to feed. Man's mind was made to receive light, and it is their joy to be in the dark; it was made capable of believing, and their glory is to be doubting. Man's heart was created for the highest good, the most enduring joys, and their loftiest ambition is to study the secrets of gas and steam, and the colors and lines of the spectrum. The secrets of that spiritual world to which their souls belong are of no account to them, and the only knowledge they value is that material science which can make their brief existence here most comfortable. Fit offshoots are they of a materialistic age which has discovered that man is only a cultivated monkey. Those who believe that they owe their manhood to something better than can be found in a baboon's progress to perfection, and who feel that they are made for something higher, must look to other teachers. Farewell.

Yours truly,
C. A. WALWORTH.

APPENDIX

ON THE UNANIMOUS TESTIMONY OF ALL AGES AND ALL RACES TO THE DOCTRINE OF HELL.

I. MODERN TESTIMONY.

THROUGHOUT all the nations which our geographies set down as enlightened, the Christian religion in some form prevails, including one-fourth of the human race. Whatever other differences are found among them, they all agree in their belief in everlasting rewards and punishments. A little school of infidels and rationalists forms the only exception.

About one-eighth of mankind are Mohammedan—Arabs, Turks, Persians, Afghans, Egyptians, Moors, etc., scattered over Asia, Asia Minor, Africa, and the eastern parts of Europe. All these believe in eternal punishments. It is taught in the Koran at long and at large.

The followers of Brahminism, with its offshoot Buddhism, including vast populations in Hindostan, Thibet, China, and all the southern countries of Asia, believe also in future rewards and punishments.

The Hindoo hell is presided over by Yama, the judge of the dead. Brahminism, in our day, admits several hells, or degrees of punishment, for the same sinner, by way of purification, which would seem to conflict with the idea of *everlasting* punishment; but this has grown out of the comparatively modern theory of metempsychosis, or soul-wandering, no mention of which theory occurs in the ancient Vedas, or sacred books. (See "Amer. Cyclop.," Brahma.)

The same essential belief in hell is found among all the barbarous nations of the earth—the Esquimaux, Greenlanders, and Kamschatkans of the North —among the New Zealanders, Feejeeans, and other islanders of the Pacific, as well as the negroes of Africa, and the red men of America. (See the various authors quoted by Alger in his "History of the Doctrine of a Future State.") In fine, this doctrine is found among all the various races of heathen, so far as their grade of intelligence will allow them to reflect upon anything beyond their animal necessities. Of the native Africans, Alger says: "They seem to believe that the souls of dead men take rank with good or bad spirits, as they have themselves been good or bad in this life." And he quotes Wilson as follows: "A native African would as soon doubt his present as his future state of being" (Wilson's "West Africa," ch. xii.)

The early colonists who first settled in this Western World found the native red men agreeing in this belief with the races of the Old World. "The Mexicans imagined three separate states of existence in the future. The wicked were to expiate their sins in everlasting darkness" ("Amer. Cyclop.," Mexico). Of the Florida Indians, and those of Peru and of the whole empire of the Incas, Garcilaso de la Vega says : " All these peoples believe in an immortal soul, and in another world where the good are crowned with glory, and recompensed for their good actions, and the wicked are punished for their crimes" ("Hist. de la Conquête de la Floride," traduit par Richelet, l. 3. ch. xi. In the original Spanish, the citation will be found in book v., 2d part, ch. ii.) The more northerly tribes of the United States and Canada had various ways of picturing the "happy hunting-grounds" and the fate of the wicked, but their doctrine was always in substance the same. Sometimes the wicked, unable to reach the Island of the Blessed, are drowned in their canoes beneath the raging waves (Schoolcraft's "Indian in his Wigwam," p. 80). Some placed their paradise in a temperate country to the south, while the bad wander about in misery, and the loud howlings of wild animals at night were believed to be their wailings (O'Callaghan's " Doc. Hist. of New York," vol. iv. Description of the New Netherlands). Others located their future world in the West, called by the Iroquois the Land of Ancestors or of Souls, which could only be reached by a long and painful journey. There the wicked are separated from the rest, and made to bear the punishment of their crimes (Père Lafitau, "Mœurs des Sauvages Amer.," tom i. ch. iv. Paris, 1724. See also Letter of P. Debrebeuf, "Relat. des Jesuites," pour l'an 1636, 2d part, ch. ii. p. 75). For the doctrine of the Natchez nation, see Letter of Father Le Petit, Kipp's "Jesuit Missions," p. 270.

The following summary of the Indian doctrine of the future state is given by Schoolcraft in his "Travels in the Mississippi Valley," ch. xviii. p. 397 (Harper's Ed., 1825):

"The Indians do not regard the approach of death with horror. Deists in religion, they look upon it as a change of state which is mainly for the better. It is regarded as the close of a series of wanderings and hardships which must sooner or later cease, which it is desirable should not take place until old age, but which, happen when it may, if it puts a period to their worldly enjoyments, also puts a period to their miseries. Most of them look to an existence in a future state, and expect to lead a happier life in another sphere. And they are not without the idea of rewards and punishments. But what this happiness is to be, where it is to be enjoyed, and what is to be the nature of the rewards and punishments, does not appear to be definitely fixed in the minds of any. If a man dies, it is said, 'He has gone to the happy land before us; he has outrun us in the race, but we shall soon follow.'

"They handle their dead without apparent emotion. After the body has been dressed in the best clothing possessed by the deceased, or the most costly and valuable that can be furnished by the relatives or friends, a funeral address is pronounced over it. This pious office is generally performed by some relative, or aged person of sense and discretion who is versed in their ancient customs and traditions. The deceased is addressed as if still living, and capable of hearing and understanding what is said.

"You have reached, says the orator, the place of sleep before us; but we shall soon lie down with you. You are going to another country, which we trust you will find pleasant. But in your journey thither, you will have to be very cautious how you travel, for your path is beset with dangers. There is one place in particular where you must be extremely cautious. You have a dark stream to cross, which is wide and deep, and the water runs rapidly. There is but a single tree lying across it, and you will be compelled to cross over it without the help of a staff.

"My brother, if your actions have been pleasing to the Great Spirit in this world, if you have been a good man in your tribe, you will get safely over; but if not, you will surely fall into the stream.

"We shall not allow you to leave us without an attendant, and a part of the provisions you have left in your lodge. At such a time (naming it) and at such a place (naming it) I killed one of our enemies, and took his scalp. He is my slave. He will henceforward be yours. You will meet him on your way, and must bid him follow you. He will cut wood and make fire for you at night; he will hunt and provide for you on the way, and render you every assistance which is necessary for the comfort of your perilous journey. We will also lay by you your gun and tomahawk for your slave to use, and your small kettle in which he will boil your corn. This wooden dish contains some provisions for you to eat at the commencement of your journey. We also kill your dog, who will follow you."

[For descriptions in detail of this future world, or Pays des Ames, of the deities who preside there, and the occupations of its inhabitants, see the above-cited work of Père Lafitau. Also the legend of "The White Stone Canoe," related by Schoolcraft, "Indian in his Wigwam."]

Thus widely scattered over the earth, separated often by wide oceans, and speaking languages unintelligible to each other, civilized or savage, the voices of the various nations and tribes unite and proclaim the existence of hell to be the belief of mankind And yet, thus far, we have only the sentiment of our own age and of the existing forms of belief. How overwhelming, this unanimity becomes when on through all the corridors of history the generations of the past send down their testimony to the same doctrine!

II. ANCIENT TESTIMONY.

It cannot be necessary to dwell upon the doctrine of the ancient Hebrews, so clearly given in their sacred books. The word hell is used by them indifferently to express any state after death. Thus, it means either the grave, the world of departed souls generally, the temporary abode of the souls of the patriarchs and other just men in waiting for the Messiah, or, finally, the hell of the damned. It is not the single word, but the combination of words and the context, which must determine the meaning. Passages abound in the Old Testament which refer to punishments after death, and those punishments eternal.

The doctrine of the ancient Greeks is beyond all doubt. I have already quoted Plato. The eternity of hell, according to their doctrine, is thus expressed by Plutarch in his "Morals," vol. iii., in the tract entitled "Whether it Were Rightly Said—Live Concealed," § 7: "In very truth, the sole punishment of ill-livers is an inglorious obscurity or a final abolition which through oblivion hurls and plunges them into deplorable rivers, bottomless seas, and a dark abyss, involving all in uselessness and inactivity, absolute ignorance and obscurity, as their last and eternal doom."

Every school-boy who has read the sixth book of the "Æneid" knows what the Romans believed, and has before his mind Virgil's gloomy picture of Tartarus, and the river of hell, Phlegethon, and of that rock "where sits, and to eternity shall sit, the unhappy Theseus."

The ancient Egyptians held the same belief: "The existence of the spirit after death was believed, and a future state of rewards and punishments inculcated, in which the good dwelt with the gods, while the wicked were consigned to fiery torments amid perpetual darkness" ("Amer. Cyclop.," Egypt). We find this belief represented on the royal tombs of Egypt. Here are delineated the solemn scenes of the judgment, the Judge, the scales of justice, and the record; there the souls of the wicked appear exposed to torments of fire and steel (Rosellini, "Mon. Civ." iii. pp. 323, 328, quoted in Kenrick's "Anc. Egypt," i. p. 409). "There is reason to believe," says Wilkinson, "from the monuments, that the souls which underwent transmigration were those of men whose sins were of a sufficiently moderate kind to admit of that purification, the unpardonable sinner being condemned to eternal fire" (Ancient Egyptians," vol. ii. p. 380).

Our Saxon ancestors, with all the ancient inhabitants of Iceland, Denmark, Sweden, and Norway, believed in an everlasting hell, as is shown by their sacred book, the Edda ("Amer. Cyclop.," Edda). The same belief is attributed to other primitive nations whose religion is partly known from books or monuments; but the proper authorities are not accessible to me at this moment. (For the Etruscans and Chaldeans, or ancient Persians, see Alger, " Doct. of Fut. State.") It is a rich field of enquiry this, but hard to complete where time and space are limited. Let me sum up the argument in a few words:

From whence comes this wondrous concurrence of mankind in all ages and of various races in the same doctrine? Either it is a general tradition having its source in one primeval revelation, or rather it is the testimony of nature, the voice of conscience, which speaks always the same language because it is the same nature, and cannot lose those intuitions which God imparted to it at the beginning, and which constitute an essential part of its life. In either case, this unanimity is an unanswerable proof of the doctrine.

www.ingramcontent.com/pod-product-compliance
Lightning Source LLC
Chambersburg PA
CBHW030349170426
43202CB00010B/1300